Studies in Natural Language Processing

Planning English sentences

Studies in Natural Language Processing
Executive Editor: Aravind K. Joshi

This series publishes monographs, texts, and edited volumes within the interdisciplinary field of computational linguistics. Sponsored by the Association for Computational Linguistics, the series will represent the range of topics of concern to the scholars working in this increasingly important field, whether their background is in formal linguistics, psycholinguistics, cognitive psychology or artificial intelligence.

Also in this series:
Natural language parsing, edited by David R. Dowty, Lauri Karttunen and Arnold Zwicky
Text generation by Kathleen R. McKeown

Planning English sentences

DOUGLAS E. APPELT

SRI International, Menlo Park, California

The right of the
University of Cambridge
to print and sell
all manner of books
was granted by
Henry VIII in 1534.
The University has printed
and published continuously
since 1584.

CAMBRIDGE UNIVERSITY PRESS

CAMBRIDGE

LONDON   NEW YORK   NEW ROCHELLE

MELBOURNE   SYDNEY

Published by the Press Syndicate of the University of Cambridge
The Pitt Building, Trumpington Street, Cambridge CB2 1RP
32 East 57th Street, New York, NY 10022, USA
10 Stamford Road, Oakleigh, Melbourne 3166, Australia

First published 1985

Printed in Great Britain at the University Press, Cambridge

Library of Congress catalogue card number: 85-47622

British Library Cataloguing in Publication Data

Appelt, Douglas E.
Planning English sentences. – (Studies in
natural language processing)
1. English language – Data processing
I. Title   II. Series
420'.1'513   PE1074.5

ISBN 0 521 30115 7

Contents

Preface

This book is based on research I did in the Stanford University Computer Science Department for the degree of Doctor of Philosophy. I express my sincere gratitude to my dissertation reading committee: Terry Winograd, Gary Hendrix, Doug Lenat and Nils Nilsson. Their discussion and comments contributed greatly to the research reported here. Barbara Grosz's thoughtful comments on my thesis contributed significantly to the quality of the research. I also thank Phil Cohen and Bonnie Webber for providing detailed comments on the first draft of this book and for providing many useful suggestions, and Aravind Joshi for his efforts in editing the Cambridge University Press *Studies in Natural Language Processing* series.

This research was supported by the Office of Naval Research under contract N00014-80-C-0296, and by the National Science Foundation under grant MCS-8115105. The preparation of this book was in part made possible by a gift from the System Development Foundation to SRI International as part of a coordinated research effort with the Center for the Study of Language and Information at Stanford University.

This book would be totally unreadable were it not for the efforts of SRI International Senior Technical Editor Savel Kliachko, who transformed my muddled ramblings into golden prose. The typesetting for this book was done using LATEX, designed by Leslie Lamport, who also provided me with much useful advice.

Nils Nilsson was director of the Artificial Intelligence Center at SRI International during the period covering this research and much of the writing of this book. I take this opportunity to thank him, and all the other people who work there, for providing the best research environment you will find anywhere in the world.

x

1

Introduction

1.1 Toward a theory of language generation and communication

A primary goal of natural-language generation research in artificial intelligence is to design a system that is capable of producing utterances with the same fluency as that of a human speaker. One could imagine a "Turing Test" of sorts in which a person was presented with a dialogue between a human and a computer and, on the basis of the naturalness of its use of the English language, asked to identify which participant was the computer. Unfortunately, no natural-language generation system yet developed can pass the test for an extended dialogue.

A language-generation system capable of passing this test would obviously have a great deal of syntactic competence. It would be capable of using correctly and appropriately such syntactic devices as conjunction and ellipsis; it would be competent at fitting its utterances into a discourse, using pronominal references where appropriate, choosing syntactic structures consistent with the changing focus, and giving an overall feeling of coherence to the discourse. The system would have a large knowledge base of basic concepts and commonsense knowledge so that it could converse about any situation that arose naturally in its domain.

However, even if a language-generation system met all the above criteria, it might still not be able to pass our "Turing Test" because to know only about the syntactic and semantic rules of the language is not enough. For this reason, calling such a system a "language-generation system" is in truth a misnomer, because it would be more accurately called a *communication* system. One must constantly bear in mind that language behavior is part of a coherent plan and is directed

1

toward satisfying the speaker's goals. Furthermore, sentences are not straightforward actions that satisfy only a single goal. The utterances people produce are crafted with great sophistication to satisfy multiple goals at different communicative levels. For example, in a single utterance a speaker may inform a hearer of two or more propositions, make a request, shift the focus of the discourse, and flatter the hearer. On the surface, this does not argue that anything more than the above criteria is needed to produce natural-sounding utterances — all that is necessary is to allow for greater complexity. Things are not that straightforward, however, because recognizing how an utterance satisfies multiple goals often requires that the hearer know about the speaker's plan, and reason about how the utterance fits into it. A speaker attempting to plan such an utterance must reason about what the hearer knows and how the hearer can interpret the speaker's intentions. When a speaker produces an utterance, he is reasoning not only about his language, but about the entire communicative process.

Consider the situation in Figure 1.1, which is typical of two agents cooperating on a task in which one has to make a request of the other. The speaker points to one of the tools on the table and says, "Use the wheelpuller to remove the flywheel." The hearer, who is observing the speaker while he makes the request, and knows that the speaker is drawing his attention to a particular tool, thinks to himself, "Ah, so that's a wheelpuller. I was wondering how I was going to get that flywheel off."

In this situation, the speaker's utterance affects the hearer far beyond a simple analysis of the propositional content of the utterance. Most obviously, the speaker is requesting the hearer to carry out a particular action, since the use of the imperative strongly suggests that a request is intended. However, the speaker includes using the wheelpuller as part of his request. If he knew that the hearer did not know that he was supposed to use the wheelpuller to remove the flywheel, then his utterance also serves to inform the hearer of what tool to use for the task. In addition, the fact that the speaker *points* to a particular object communicates his intention to refer to it with the noun phrase "the wheelpuller." (In fact, pointing may be the only way to refer successfully to an object when the only mutually believed description of it is that it is some sort of thing.) Since the intention to

2

refer has been communicated, the noun phrase also communicates the fact that the intended referent is a wheelpuller. Thus the speaker has performed a "labeling" action that will enable him to refer more easily to the object in subsequent utterances. The speaker could have just said, "Use *that thing* to remove the flywheel," if he had no goal of informing the hearer that the tool was a wheelpuller.

Utterances that are intended by the speaker to satisfy multiple goals are very common. Here are a few examples of common situations in which the speaker plans an utterance to satisfy multiple goals:

- A rock climber says to a friend, "Joe and I are going to climb the Snake Dike Route on Half Dome next weekend." The speaker does not use the prepositional phrase "on Half Dome" to pick out a particular Snake Dike Route from several that he and the hearer mutually know about. Most likely, he is informing the hearer that he is going to climb a particular route, and the additional descriptor "on Half Dome" is intended to inform the hearer of the location of a route that he never heard of before, and perhaps impress him as well.

Figure 1.1: Satisfying multiple goals with a request

- The rabidly anti-American Ayatollah Khomeini says "The Great Satan shall not defeat us." It is obvious from the context of the utterance that the description "Great Satan" is intended to refer to the United States, even though the description is not objectively true of its intended referent. In this case, the speaker exploits a noun phrase to simultaneously refer and communicate his emotional attitude toward the referent.

- Multiple-goal satisfaction even plays a role in such conventional utterances as "Could you tell me what time it is?" In this case the speaker chooses the indirect speech act to satisfy a goal of demonstrating politeness toward the hearer, although the more direct but less polite "What time is it?" would have conveyed the request equally well.

1.2 The need for a general planning mechanism

Figure 1.1 illustrates how understanding a speaker's physical actions can be important for understanding an utterance. The speaker's action of grasping the wheelpuller is interpreted by the hearer to have communicative intent, like pointing. The speaker assumes that the hearer knows the connection between such communicative gestures and the linguistic act of uttering an noun phrase. Since linguistic acts and physical acts can be interpreted together in reasoning about a speaker's intentions, a language-generation system that treats physical and linguistic actions as uniformly as possible will enable the production of utterances that, like the one in Figure 1.1, satisfy multiple goals.

In Figure 1.2 the agents are faced with a problem similar to that of Figure 1.1, but the agent making the request happens to be holding a large box, which prevents him from grasping the wheelpuller as he did in Figure 1.1. If he says the same thing as he did in Figure 1.1 to achieve realization of his request, he will not succeed; since the hearer does not know what a wheelpuller is, the speaker will not have established his intention to refer, as he did in the previous example.

One option open to the speaker is to devise some description of the object that does not require pointing, and perhaps to inform the hearer later in a different utterance that the object is a wheelpuller. However, since the only mutually believed descriptors of the intended referent are those resulting from perception, the resulting description will probably be awkward (e.g., "the thing with two arms and a large screw in the middle"). The speaker could also attempt to describe the object first and then refer to it; however, this tactic too can be awkward. Of course, if an agent does not have physical actions at his disposal, these techniques are his only alternatives.

Another alternative that could be planned when the speaker has both physical and linguistic actions at his disposal is for him to set down the box, which would free his hands, and then proceed as in Figure 1.1. As this example illustrates, relatively low-level linguistic planning, such as deciding what description to use to refer to something, can lead to the planning of physical actions. Such interaction provides support for the argument in favor of closely correlating the planning of physical and linguistic actions.

Many communicative situations arise in which the speaker and the hearer are not in proximity to each other, and therefore physical actions are not relevant to the planning process. A common example is the writing of text, whereby the reader who will interpret the text is not only normally unknown to the writer, but will almost certainly be at a different location. In such a case, a model of

Figure 1.2: The need for integrating physical and linguistic actions

language generation based on planning is still applicable because, even though there is really just one agent, the writer must still plan his text as though there were another agent directly involved. Instead of reasoning about a particular person's beliefs, a "typical reader" is assumed to be the other agent, and all the problems of intention communication and reasoning about the beliefs of the typical reader are likely to apply. Considerations such as his knowledge of the topic and his technical sophistication come into play.

A hypothesis of this research is that an agent's behavior is controlled by a general goal satisfaction process. Agents are assumed to have goals that are satisfied by constructing plans from available actions. Given that an agent's overall behavior is controlled by such a planning process, it is advantageous for his linguistic behavior to be controlled by such a process as well. The reasons for this conclusion are that (1) agents have to plan *both* physical and linguistic actions to achieve their goals, (2) linguistic and physical actions interact with each other, and (3) actions such as informing and requesting interact and can be realized simultaneously in the same utterance. Since a language-generation system must reason about these interactions to produce natural-sounding utterances, a uniform process that plans both physical and linguistic actions is needed.

1.3   A theory of language generation based on planning

Generating natural language by means of a general planning mechanism is a reasonable approach to the problem for a variety of reasons discussed in the previous section. However, this approach requires adopting a different view of language and communication from the one that has usually been characterized in past language-generation research. Many previous theories and their related systems have regarded language processing in a manner analogous to that depicted in Figure 1.3, which illustrates a view that has been labeled the *conduit metaphor* by Reddy (1979). The conduit metaphor refers to the treatment of language as a pipeline or conduit that relays information from the speaker to the hearer. The speaker, starting with some idea of what he wants to say, "packages" it in natural language and sends the package through the conduit to the hearer, who then unwraps the package and removes the contents. This metaphor is quite pervasive in our commonsense intuitions about language and is reflected in many of our prevalent sayings, for example "He got his ideas across very well," or "He couldn't put his thoughts into words."

The disadvantage of this general view is that it forces one to postulate a very strong separation between two stages of the utterance-planning process: deciding *what* to say and deciding *how* to say it. Most language-generation research to date has adopted the what-how separation as a design principle to be saliently reflected in the structure of systems to be designed. Usually there is an "expert system" which draws upon a very large corpus of knowledge about its task domain when interacting with a user. When the expert system needs to communicate, it encodes a fragment of its knowledge in some internal language and then passes it on to a "generation module" that translates the message from the internal language into English.

In contrast to the language-as-conduit view outlined above, the approach advocated by this theory (represented in Figure 1.4) treats language not as something to be transferred through a conduit, but rather as a set of actions available to agents that affects the mental states of other agents. This approach regards decisions about "what to say" and "how to say it" as two facets of the same overall

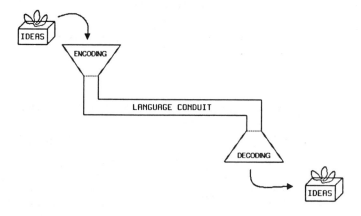

Figure 1.3: The conduit metaphor

process, and recognizes the interactions between them. The planning of an action appropriate for a given situation necessitates consideration of several crucial elements: different kinds of goals that are satisfied by utterances; the knowledge of the hearer; general knowledge about the world; the constraints imposed by the syntax of the language. The utterance planner can integrate these diverse knowledge sources to arrive at a plan involving abstract specifications of speech acts and then, finally, produce English sentences. Instead of regarding the hearer as the mere consumer of a message, the utterance planner treats him as an active participant in the communication process.

The planning system developed as a part of this research is called KAMP, which is an acronym for **K**nowledge **A**nd **M**odalities **P**lanner. KAMP is a hierarchical-planning system that uses a nonlinear representation of plans, called a *procedural network* by Sacerdoti (1977). A hierarchical design for a utterance-planning system was selected because it provides for separating the planning of domain-level goals and actions and the planning of low-level linguistic actions, as well as for intermediate levels of abstraction that facilitate the integration of multiple goals

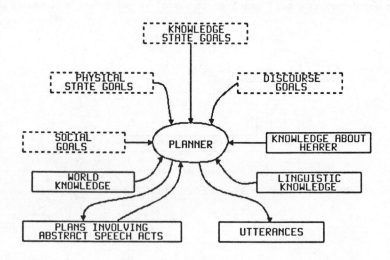

Figure 1.4: Overview of an utterance planner

8

into utterances. The hierarchy of linguistic actions used by KAMP is represented in Figure 1.5. The planner can focus its attention on domain-level and high-level linguistic actions while ignoring details about the choice of syntactic structures and descriptions for referring expressions. However, the uniformity of treatment of linguistic actions allows higher-level goals and actions to be influenced by the expansion of low-level linguistic actions. The mechanism KAMP uses to accomplish this is described in Chapter 6.

The highest-level linguistic actions are called *illocutionary acts*, which are such speech acts as informing or requesting represented at a very high level of abstraction, without any consideration given to an action's ultimate linguistic realization. The next level consists of *surface speech-acts*, which are abstract representations of sentences with particular syntactic structures. At this level, specific linguistic knowledge becomes important. One surface speech act can realize one or more illocutionary acts. The next level consists of *concept activation actions*, which

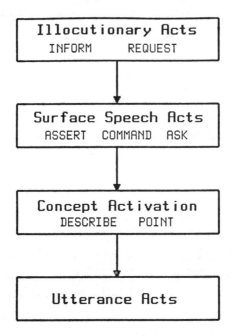

Figure 1.5: A hierarchy of actions related to language

entail the planning of descriptions that are mutually believed by both the speaker and the hearer to refer to objects in the world. Finally, concept activation actions are expanded as *utterance acts*, at which point specific words and syntactic structures are chosen to realize the descriptors chosen for the concept activation actions. These syntactic structures have to be compatible with the sentential syntactic structure selected when the surface speech act is planned. Concept activation actions can also be expanded partially as physical actions that establish the speaker's intention to refer, such as pointing. The detailed axiomatization and treatment by KAMP of each of these action types is described in detail in Chapters 5, 6 and 7.

1.4   The goals of this research

For any research to merit the label "scientific," there must be a clear idea of just what constitutes the problem that is being addressed, and what is to be regarded as a potential solution. The problem that confronts us here is essentially one of explanation of behavior. Agents are observed to exhibit consistent behavior; consequently some explanation is required to account for why they do what they do. This research accepts as given the mentalistic hypothesis that agents have mental states that causally determine their actions. What this research must explicate, at least in part, is how particular mental states account for particular actions. Since this work focuses on language, it is particularly concerned with the question of how holding a particular set of beliefs and intentions results in an agent's making a particular utterance.

Mental states are difficult objects to deal with because they are not directly observable. Therefore, this research proceeds by constructing a formal, computational theory (along with a system that embodies this theory) in which it is possible to represent mental states and provide an explicit mechanism whereby these states determine actions. To the extent that such a model can indeed account for observed behavior, one has succeeded in providing a computational theory.

To provide a complete computational theory of speech acts and the use of natural language is a very tall order, and this research falls far short of this ultimate goal. The principal significant contributions until now have been the establishment of a framework for such a complete theory, and an initial examination of the major problems in representing knowledge about knowledge, planning, the axiomatization of illocutionary acts, surface speech acts, and focusing actions so the accounts for all of them can be unified and incorporated into a single computational model.

Finally, the KAMP system is not intended to be a cognitive model. KAMP is not intended to be a psychological model of human behavior, although it may reflect some of the aspects of human language processing.

This book is divided into chapters that deal with each of the problems that must be considered in building a computational model of a language speaker. Chapter 2 reviews important related research in natural-language generation, planning and problem-solving, philosophy and linguistics. Important ideas that have influenced the development of the theory presented here are discussed. Chapter 3 is a detailed discussion of the possible-worlds-semantics approach to reasoning about knowledge, intention, and action. This chapter will contain familiar material if the reader is acquainted with Moore's approach (Moore, 1980) to reasoning about knowledge and action. Chapter 4 describes the design of the KAMP multi-agent planning system. KAMP's general features for multiple-agent planning are described here without detailed reference to its utterance-planning abilities. The reader who is interested only in KAMP's application to distributed multiagent planning can read just Chapters 3 and 4 disregarding the language-oriented chapters that follow them.

Chapter 5 describes the possible-worlds-semantics axiomatization of illocutionary acts in detail. The reader unfamiliar with Moore (1980) should read Chapter 3 first. Chapter 6 describes how KAMP plans surface linguistic acts, keeps track of the discourse focus, and plans concept-activation actions and indirect speech acts. Chapter 7 describes a complete example of utterance planning by KAMP, starting with a high-level domain goal. Chapter 8 discusses the importance of the ideas in this book as well as potential avenues of research opened up as a result of the work described.

2
An overview of related research

2.1 Introduction

The planning of natural-language utterances builds on contributions from a number of disciplines. The construction of the multiagent planning system is relevant to artificial intelligence research on planning and knowledge representation. The axiomatization of illocutionary acts discussed in Chapter 5 relies on results in speech act theory and the philosophy of language. Constructing a grammar of English builds on the study of syntax in linguistics and of semantics in both linguistics and philosophy. A complete survey of the relevant literature would go far beyond the scope of this book. This chapter is included to give the reader an overview of some of the most important research that is pertinent to utterance planning.

2.2 Language generation

It was quite a long time before the problem of language generation began to receive the attention it deserves. Beginning in about 1982, there has been a virtual explosion in the quantity of research being done in this field, and a complete review of all of it could well fill a book (see Bolc and McDonald, forthcoming). This chapter presents an overview of some of the earlier work that provides a foundation for the research that follows.

Several early language-generation systems, (e.g. Friedman, 1969), were designed more for the purpose of testing grammars than for communication. The earliest language-generation systems designed for communication depended upon ad hoc strategies that produced reasonable behavior in predictable situations. An example of such a language-generation system was Winograd's SHRDLU (1972). SHRDLU produced language by having a large set of templates with variables that could be instantiated appropriately in different instances. These templates, combined with a number of heuristics about question-answering, reference, and pronominalization, enabled the system to produce dialogues that sounded quite natural, given the simplicity of the technique. This technique is rather brittle because it cannot be extended straightforwardly to handle novel situations.

Nevertheless, since it was possible to get reasonable performance by using simple techniques, the problem of language generation was considered less interesting and urgent than that of language understanding; hence it received much less attention from researchers. Many application-oriented systems still use the template-instantiation approach, since they operate in highly restricted domains in which some generality can be sacrificed in the interest of simplifying a component that is peripheral to their primary concerns. Some well-known expert systems that have employed this technique are the explanation component of MYCIN (Scott et al., 1977), and the explanation component of Swartout's digitalis therapy advisor (Swartout, 1981).

In the early 1970s, some research was done to extend the simple approach of instantiating patterns to more general grammar-based approaches. These systems shared a reliance on a grammar of the language, usually expressed as an augmented transition network (ATN) to embody the system's linguistic knowledge. The language-generation systems accepted an input in an internal representation language (usually a semantic network fragment); a side-effect of a traversal of an ATN would be a natural-language sentence.

One of the earliest of these grammar-based generation systems was that of Simmons and Slocum (1972). The generation system used an ATN grammar that performed a function quite similar to the inverse of the recognition process, which, in their system, was also based on an ATN grammar. The language generator would be given a fragment of a semantic network to represent the propositional content of the intended utterance. The generation procedure would first isolate a node in the network fragment as the main proposition and choose a verb to express it. The generation ATN had tests on the various arcs that would query

14

features in the input data structure, together with features of the selected verb. The result of traversing an arc would be the production of a word, a clause, or a prepositional phrase. Simmons and Slocum used a set of "paraphrase rules" to relate synonymous lexical choices to the underlying semantic structure. These rules made it possible to generate both "Wellington defeated Napoleon at the Battle of Waterloo" and "Bonaparte lost the Battle of Waterloo to the Duke of Wellington." The question-answering algorithm used some simple heuristics to match the lexical choices made while constructing the answer with those made by the user of the system in asking a question, which often led to adoption of the proper lexical choices. An example of such a heuristic would be *"Use the same verb in answering the question as the speaker did in asking it."* Such a heuristic would favor generation of the second sentence above in response to the question "Who lost the Battle of Waterloo?", producing reasonable behavior without any analysis to determine how the sentence fitted into the discourse.

Simmons and Slocum's system was another example of how much can be accomplished in language generation with relatively simple techniques. However, their system embodied no notion of the way an utterance fits into a discourse other than pattern matching with the user's question. As a result, it could perform only the simplest generation of definite references. Moreover, it was designed purely as a question-answering system that never took the initiative in a dialogue.

Goldman (1974) also developed an ATN-based language-generation system that focused on a different set of issues. Simmons and Slocum deliberately chose to have a large number of primitive concepts in their representation system, thus simplifying the problem of lexical choice considerably. For theoretical reasons, Goldman assumed a knowledge representation called *conceptual dependency* (Schank, 1975) that was based on a very small number of predicates. The primary problem that he addressed was that of finding a good lexical choice that would describe a concept that was encoded in the internal representation as relationships between a large number of semantic primitives. His solution was to use a discrimination net to filter possible lexical choices.

Goldman's generator was designed as part of the question-answering component of the MARGIE system (Schank, 1975); since it was designed as a question answerer that produced responses with only a single question for a discourse context, it suffered from most of the deficiencies of the Simmons and Slocum generator.

The systems of Goldman and Simmons and Slocum are the exemplars of a number of ATN-based language-generation systems developed subsequently, including those of Wong (1975), von Hahn et al. (1980), and others.

There are two large grammar-based language-generation systems currently under development that deserve special attention because of the large body of theoretical and applied work they represent. The first is the MUMBLE system developed by McDonald (1978, 1980); the other is the NIGEL/PENMAN system developed by Mann (Mann and Matthiessen, 1983; Mann, 1983).

McDonald (1978, 1980) has developed a generation system called MUMBLE that differs significantly from both the pattern instantiation or the ATN grammar-based approaches. MUMBLE has one of the broadest coverages of the English language of any generation system developed to date. McDonald adopted the hypothesis that the best design for a language-generation system should reflect certain observations about human language production. Although the system was not constructed specifically as a psycholinguistic model, it embodies many assumptions about human language production that are used by the system to computational advantage. For example, decisions about the realization of an element of the intended utterance cannot be retracted once they have been made. McDonald claims that human language production conforms to a similar principle of determinism, with the resultant advantage of limiting the amount of processing that needs to be done to produce an utterance.

McDonald separates the language-generation process into three levels. The highest of these is the "expert system." The expert system knows about problem-solving in some domain, but does not necessarily have to know anything about language. The lowest level (the one realized by MUMBLE) is the "linguistic component," which knows about English grammar, has a lexicon appropriate to the application domain, and processes some information about the intended audience. McDonald also proposes an intermediate level called the "speaker component," which acts as an interface between the expert system and the linguistic component. The speaker component knows what the expert system wants to say, knows what kinds of data structures are expected by the linguistic component, and encodes an appropriate message to be passed to the latter for generation.

Language generation is a two-phase process. The first phase expands the message into a tree representing the surface syntactic structure of the utterance. The second phase traverses the tree built by the first phase, printing words, annotating the grammatical context, recording the history of the process, and propagating grammatical constraints.

The majority of the work in MUMBLE is done by procedurally encoded rules in the grammar and lexicon. These procedures, which are invoked by the controller at appropriate times while traversing the syntactic-structure tree under construction, determine what would be the best realization of a particular message element within its context. In addition they query the discourse state and audience model to ascertain the best options in making decisions about such issues as pronominalization and in choosing among syntactic structures.

Although MUMBLE's coverage of the English language is extensive and encompasses some discourse phenomena (e.g., it has reasonable heuristics for pronominalization and definite reference), it does have certain limitations. Since it has the advantage of being portable between disparate expert systems, which may use different knowledge representations, it does not have its own world model to reason with. The effect of reasoning with a world model is obtained when the system implementer writes grammar routines that are capable of invoking the expert system's knowledge in their decision procedures. MUMBLE has served as the basis for several recent research projects that extend its capabilities in various ways (Conklin and McDonald, 1982; Cook, Lehnert, and McDonald, 1984).

Mann (Mann and Moore, 1979; Matthiessen, 1981; Mann, 1983) has developed a language-generation system called PENMAN. It has several modules: *acquisition* to acquire from an external system a body of information that is to be communicated, *text planning* to organize a discourse, *sentence generation* to generate the text and *improvement* to criticize and improve the text after it is produced. As of this writing, most of the work has been expended on the sentence generation module and its associated grammar, NIGEL. The NIGEL grammar is an extensive *systemic grammar* (Berry, 1975, 1977; Halliday and Tastin, 1981) and a collection

17

of *realization procedures* that translate systemic features into syntactic structures. The generation module works by proceeding through the systemic network and making choices in each of the feature systems; once all the features have been selected, the realization component produces the utterance. Each choice system has a procedure associated with it called a *chooser*, which invokes a collection of domain- and representation-specific routines that provide answers to questions about the domain and information needed to build the plan for the intended utterance.

Some current research projects are actively investigating other issues in language generation. One such project is that of McKeown (1982), who is concentrating on the problem of generating multisentence responses to queries about a database schema. McKeown's basic approach is to define a number of organizational schemata such as *compare and contrast, illustrate by example,* and *analogy,* and to use rules associated with each schema to incorporate relevant information into a coherent text. Mann and Moore (1979) have also done some work in organizing a large corpus of knowledge into coherent text by dividing a scenario into a sequence of problem-solving stages that deal with the scenario at different levels of abstraction. They have developed a system called KDS that embodies this theory. Mann and Matthiessen (1984) have developed a theory of rhetorical structure schemata that attempts to classify different discourse strategies in a manner more general than that of McKeown.

2.3   Goals and plans: Their influence on utterances

The early work in artificial intelligence on the relationship of plans and goals to language was done not in the area of generation, but rather in the area of understanding. Bruce (1975) carried out some of the initial research that set the stage for true speech-act planning. He started from the viewpoint that language is purposeful behavior, and that the task of comprehending a sentence is not only a process of recovering its meaning, but also of interpreting the speaker's intentions in producing it. Bruce proposed developing a computational formalism for representing an agent's beliefs and describing actions such as speech acts that affect beliefs. The formalism was never developed to the point where it was actually implemented in a working system, but the basic direction taken in his research was nonetheless important.

Recent work in the understanding of simple stories (Schank, 1977) has recognized the need for reasoning about the underlying intentions of agents. Much early work on the understanding of stories relied on matching events in them with some stereotypical sequence of actions called a "script." It was soon realized that it was impossible to capture every possible sequence of events beforehand, and that some general mechanism of understanding the plans of the agents involved was essential. A model was developed in which agents could plan various actions, including asking and telling. The model was used to understand stories about agents' attainment their goals (Wilensky, 1978).

Meehan (Schank, 1977) extended these early ideas about planning to the design of a system that produced simple stories. Meehan's system was not a language-generation program since it did not produce any actual English sentences. What it did was to compose formal descriptions of short stories about different agents who made plans to achieve their goals and could be frustrated by various situations and events. The agent's plans included actions of telling, asking, and persuading.

Allen, Cohen and Perrault have done considerable work in extending the ideas of Bruce (1975) by developing implementable formalisms that were incorporated in working systems for the planning and recognition of speech acts (Allen, 1978; Allen and Perrault, 1978; Cohen, 1978; Cohen and Perrault, 1979). This research, unlike the earlier work that inferred plans behind the actions of agents, assumed that speech acts work through *intended plan recognition* rather than merely as a result of agents figuring out what other agents are trying to do. This enabled a number of intention-recognition heuristics and a rigorous speech act theory to be developed. Allen (1978) designed a system that would understand indirect speech acts by attempting to recognize the speaker's plan and then trying to determine how the utterance could fit into that plan. Cohen (1978) is concerned with the problem of producing an appropriate speech act to satisfy a speaker's goal. Cohen implemented a system called OSCAR that can plan for a hearer to recognize the speaker's intention to perform a speech act, and thereby succeed in informing him or requesting something of him. Cohen's system produces a specification of the speech act that names the type of action to be performed, the agent, and the propositional content of the act, but does not actually produce English sentences.

The utterance planning research reported herein, as well as such other speech act planning work as that of Allen, Cohen, and Perrault, was tested in domains that are fundamentally task-oriented — e.g., as in performing some cooperative problem-solving task or assisting a customer at an information booth. This work leaves open the question as to whether planning and problem-solving techniques are also useful in less well-structured domains. Hobbs and Evans (1980) examine the goal structure in a "small talk" dialogue and conclude that in fact they are. The goals that arise are of a different nature — more social goals are involved for which formal description is difficult. Nevertheless, careful examination reveals the same goal directed behavior as is apparent in the more well-structured domains.

2.4 Planning, problem solving, and knowledge representation

Since this book is about *planning* utterances, this review would not be complete without acknowledging the debt owed to previous research in planning and problem solving. The planning system described in Chapter 4 builds on ideas embodied in the early systems described below.

STRIPS (Fikes, 1971) was one of the first planning systems. It can be characterized as using a first order logic description of states of the world, with an extralogical set of operators that would add and delete assertions from the world model. The basic control strategy was backward-chaining from a partially specified goal state.

Kowalski (Kowalski, 1974) demonstrated that it was not only possible to formalize planning entirely within logic, but that with appropriate constraints on the axioms, planning could be carried out through normal deduction procedures with about the same complexity as the STRIPS approach.

The next major advance in planning was the encoding of planning operators in a hierarchy of abstraction, as advocated by Sacerdoti (Sacerdoti, 1977). It seems intuitively plausible that the space a planner has to search could be reduced significantly if it could form a rough plan first, using abstract operators, later refining it into a more concrete low-level plan. "Critic" procedures would be employed to detect and repair what would presumably be easily-resolved inconsistencies arising at the lower level.

Of course, there is no guarantee that the structure of the high-level plan would look anything at all like the final low-level plan; moreover, this approach would work only for problems that were nearly decomposable, i.e. there are minimal interactions between the subproblems. It is strictly an empirical fact that this property holds for a large number of planning domains. In spite of this shortcoming, it appears that hierarchical planning has wide applicability in many areas, including utterance planning. Much current planning research deals with the problems that arise in circumventing the interactions that ensue between actions in a plan and that involve chosing among instantiations of variables in the plan. Such ideas as Stefik's "constraint posting" (Stefik, 1980) and Hayes-Roth's "opportunistic planning" (Hayes-Roth, 1979) are attempts to solve some of these problems. An excellent review of different robot planning systems and the types of problems they can and cannot handle can be found in Nilsson (1980).

The knowledge representation used by the language-planning system for reasoning about what agents know owes much to the research of Moore (1980). Before Moore, most systems that had to reason about propositional attitudes did so with overly simplistic and ad hoc techniques, since solution of such reasoning problems was not the primary goal of the research. Moore's work on a possible-worlds-semantics approach to reasoning about knowledge, belief, and action is the first to be directed primarily toward that end. This work and some alternative related approaches are summarized in detail in Chapter 3.

2.5 Philosophy and linguistics

Research in philosophy and linguistics has provided the foundation upon which this work is built. The view of language production as a planning process owes much to Austin and Searle's development of speech act theory (Austin, 1962; Searle, 1969, 1979a), which views utterances as actions performed by speakers to achieve intended effects. Searle attempted to elaborate on this view by specifying explicit preconditions and effects for different types of speech acts. One of Searle's

21

major contributions was to establish the importance of recognition of intention in the production and understanding of speech acts. This work is discussed in greater detail in Chapter 5.

Grice (1975) discussed the problems of analyzing *implicatures* — situations in which a speaker's utterance does not convey his intentions literally, but rather his intended meaning is to be inferred from the literal meaning. Grice focuses his analysis on *conversational implicatures,* which are implicatures in which the intended meaning is recovered by reliance on several *cooperative principles* of conversational behavior. Some of the strategies employed by KAMP such as action subsumption instantiate these maxims.

Levy (1979a, 1979b) uses concepts of communicative goals and strategies to develop a framework for analyzing natural spoken discourse. He extends this formulation (Levy, 1979b) and proposes for the production of text a "production model" and an "artifact thesis" that join together many previous attempts in different disciplines to describe discourse. The research reported in this thesis may be viewed in part as an attempt to formalize the integration of some of the multiple perspectives described by Levy.

The idea that utterances are part of a speaker's plans to achieve his goals has appeared in the linguistics literature under different guises for quite some time. A number of modern linguists, looking at language beyond its properties as a formal symbol system, have examined questions relating to the way language is used and evolves within a sociocultural setting to serve a variety of functions. Halliday (1978) has advocated breaking away from a view of language exclusively as an information conduit; he emphasizes the importance of all language functions and how a speaker utilizes them in various settings. Linguists who have worked in the context of speech act theory (e.g., Bierwisch, Cole, Gordon, Grice, Kiefer, Lakoff, and Morgan, to name but a few) have established a theoretical foundation for the linguistic component of utterance planning. The considerable amount of empirical data considered by them provides a set of phenomena against which to test the adequacy of a plan-based theory of language.

3
Representing knowledge about intensional concepts

3.1 Introduction

This chapter examines some of the special requirements of a knowledge representation formalism that arise from the planning of linguistic actions. Utterance planning requires the ability to reason about a wide variety of *intensional concepts* that include knowledge per se, mutual knowledge, belief, and intention. Intensional concepts can be represented in intensional logic by operators that apply to both individuals and sentences. What makes intensional operators different from ordinary extensional ones such as conjunction and disjunction is that one cannot substitute terms that have the same truth-value within the scope of one of these operators without sometimes changing the truth-value of the entire sentence. For example, suppose that John knows Mary's phone number. Suppose that unbeknown to John, Mary lives with Bill — and therefore Bill's phone number is the same as Mary's. It does not follow from these premises that John knows what Bill's phone number is.

The planning of linguistic actions requires reasoning about several different types of intensional operators. In this research we shall be concerned with the operators **Know** (and occasionally the related operator **Believe**), **Mutually-Know**, **Knowref** (knowing the denotation of a description), **Intend** (intending to make a proposition true) and **Intend-To-Do** (intending to perform a particular action). In addition to reasoning about what agents know and intend, it is necessary to plan *actions* that affect an agent's knowledge and intentions. For this reason, a

23

formal system is required that facilitates reasoning about all of these concepts simultaneously.

This chapter describes a knowledge representation that is based on a possible-worlds semantics for a modal logic, is adequate for representing the knowledge needed by a cooperative agent to participate in task-oriented dialogues, and is capable of being used in an efficient manner by existing first-order-logic deduction systems. This possible-worlds-semantics approach and its integration into a first-order-logic deduction system was developed by Moore (1980). Moore's theory has been extended to deal with cases of intention and mutual knowledge that were not considered by him; otherwise Moore's approach has been adopted essentially intact. Since an understanding of the overall approach is a prerequisite for understanding the KAMP utterance-planning system and the axiomatization of illocutionary acts, both Moore's basic approach and the extensions that have been adopted are described in this chapter.

Each of the concepts of knowledge, belief, and intention discussed in this chapter has provided fuel for centuries of philosophical debate. It is not our purpose here to settle issues such as determining when true belief constitutes knowledge, or even to advance opinions regarding them. Moore's representation is neutral with respect to most of these issues. However, the representation is intended to provide sufficient generality and flexibility to enable the designer of a system using the representation to adopt whatever philosophical perspective on these issues he deems appropriate to the situation. This research takes a pragmatic approach to most of these issues, making assumptions that lead to the simplest system that behaves reasonably in task-oriented dialogues.

The central problem of knowledge representation is that of finding a suitable set of axioms to express facts about the world and then to draw the appropriate inferences from them. To that end, all the axioms will be expressed in the notation of an intensional logic with operators for knowledge, belief, mutual knowledge, and intention. The semantics for all of these operators are readily expressible in first order predicate calculus with equality. The representation is intended to be independent of any details of implementation.

The axioms employed by KAMP assume that the theorem prover is capable of using axiom schemata and that it is capable of utilizing simple control information governing whether rules are used in a forward or backward direction during deduction and some syntactic restrictions on the terms that can unify with a term of the rule. These restrictions are necessary to prevent the theorem prover from looping endlessly in certain cases. However, issues of control and efficiency extending beyond this fundamental level are outside the scope of this research.

3.2   Approaches to reasoning about knowledge and belief

The problem of reasoning about intensional concepts has been the focus of much recent research in artificial intelligence. There has been work on reasoning about knowledge and belief (Konolige, 1980, 1984; Moore, 1980, McCarthy et al., 1978, McCarthy, 1979; Perlis, 1981) as well as on related concepts such as permission and obligation (McCarty, 1983). This research does not seek to contribute substantially to this body of knowledge, but, since reasoning about intensional concepts is central to utterance planning, this research must draw heavily upon previous contributions, making extensions wherever necessary.

Three approaches to reasoning about knowledge and belief have been discussed in the literature. They are (1) *syntactic theories* (Konolige, 1980; Perlis, 1981), (2) *the deduction belief model* (Konolige, 1984), and (3) *modal logic and possible-worlds semantics* (Moore, 1980). Each theory has advantages and disadvantages that affect its suitability as the basis of an utterance planning system.

The central distinguishing feature of a syntactic theory of belief is that there are terms in the language that denote sentences in a logical theory. Belief is axiomatized as a relation between an agent and a *sentence* (not, as one might suspect, between an agent and a proposition). Viewed intuitively, this means that an agent has a set of sentences called his *belief set,* and that the facts he believes are those that are represented either explicitly by sentences belonging to the set or implicitly by sentences that are derivable from the belief set through the application of some rules of inference.

The advantages of the syntactic theories are that they are fairly intuitive and that the assumption of *consequential closure,* (i.e. that an agent believes all logical consequences of his beliefs) can be avoided by postulating that an agent operates on his belief sentences with rules of inference that are weaker than modus ponens.

One of the difficulties of the syntactic approach is the representation of facts that an agent *does not* know, (as opposed to the propositions that are believed to be false) and assertions that an agent believes P or believes Q (as opposed to believing $P \vee Q$). These difficulties can be overcome (Konolige, 1980) by axiomatizing an agent's belief set as a first-order theory, and then axiomatizing a metatheory in which statements about the belief sets can express the problematic assertions. However, once it becomes necessary to coordinate deduction on multiple levels, or employ deduction that involves non-standard rules of inference, there is no obvious computationally efficient implementation of the resulting system.

Konolige's deduction model of belief (Konolige, 1984) is similar to the syntactic approach, but is less fraught with computational difficulties. Each agent is modeled by a *deduction structure,* which consists of a logical language along with with rules of inference. This deduction structure provides a model for a modal belief logic in which the axioms about an agent's beliefs are stated. The deduction structure is similar to the belief set in the syntactic approach, but with one crucial difference: the rules of each agent's deduction structure are actually present as a subset of the inference rules of the modal belief logic. Proofs about deduction structures in the belief logic use these rules directly in their derivation, thus eliminating the computationally disadvantageous metalanguage reflection of the syntactic approach.

The possible-worlds approach to reasoning about knowledge originated with Hintikka (1962) and was extended by Moore (1980) to integrate reasoning about knowledge and action in a single formalism. The general idea behind this approach is to axiomatize knowledge or belief as the necessity operator ($\Box$) in a modal logic, and then to axiomatize a Kripke-like possible-worlds semantics (Kripke, 1963) for the modal logic in first-order logic in which it is possible to reason using conventional first-order-logic theorem provers.

The axioms for standard modal logics are taken from the following schemata:

M1: P, where P is a tautology.

M2: $\Box (P \supset Q) \supset (\Box P \supset \Box Q)$

M3: $\Box P \supset P$

M4: $\Box P \supset \Box \Box P$

M5: $\neg \Box P \supset \Box \neg \Box P$

The modal logic that includes only Axioms M1 and M2 is called K. Adding Axiom M3 yields the modal logic T. If the modal operator $\Box$ is interpreted as **Know**, this axiom says that whatever is known must be true. Adding Axiom M4 to T yields $S4$, which provides the capability to reason that, if an agent knows P, then he knows that he knows P. Adding M5 to $S4$ yields $S5$ and the powerful introspective property that, if an agent does not know P, then he knows that he does not know P.

The modal logic used by Moore (and in this research as well) is similar to $S4$. Axiom M5 is too powerful; the resulting theory is at odds with one's commonsense intuitions about one's knowledge about one's own knowledge. Each of the calculi $S4$ and $S5$ can be weakened by the omission of Axiom M3. This is appropriate if what one is reasoning about is belief rather than knowledge.

The inference rules for standard modal logics are the familiar modus ponens and *necessitation* (if P is a theorem, then so is $\Box P$). Any modal logic that uses modus ponens and necessitation as rules of inference, and is at least as strong as K, has the following property: if $P \supset Q$ is a theorem, then so is $\Box P \supset \Box Q$. Therefore, whenever P is a theorem and an agent believes P, then he must also believe Q. One might therefore reason that, if either Fermat's Last Theorem or its negation follows from Peano's axioms, any agent who knows Peano's axioms knows whether Fermat's Last Theorem is true or false. There is no really satisfactory way of avoiding this property of logical omniscience in the possible-worlds formalism, and that is a major weakness of the approach.

In spite of this difficulty, the possible-worlds approach has been chosen as the basis of the knowledge representation for the KAMP utterance-planning system for two reasons. First, the task domain and types of sentences considered do not place sufficient demands upon the formalism for these difficulties to be a serious impediment to progress in the fundamental areas of formalizing and planning

27

speech acts. While planning and understanding speech acts requires a great deal of reasoning about what agents know, most of these inferences are obvious. In practical situations, it is not unreasonable to assume that agents have the capability of making all possible inferences because those that people are expected to make when they communicate successfully are actually almost always made (or at least agents behave as if they were). In addition, one must reason about how various actions affect what is known. Moore has worked out a very elegant application of possible-worlds formalisms to reasoning about both actions and their effects on knowledge. While the deduction model approach has an excellent prospect of overcoming the fundamental representational inadequacies of the possible-worlds approach, much work remains to be done on planning and theorem proving within that formalism. For these reasons, the possible-worlds approach is adopted, albeit its difficulties are acknowledged and deferred until future research.

3.3 Representing knowledge in the possible-worlds formalism

The key to developing any Kripke-like semantics for an intensional logic is to define the meaning of the sentential modal operators in terms of accessibility relations among possible worlds. One can then axiomatize the properties of the accessibility relations in first-order logic and, instead of reasoning about the truth of propositions, reason about the relations that hold among different possible worlds in which the propositions hold. Adopting the latter approach, the designer of an AI system can cast the entire axiomatization of the world in first-order logic and apply his well-developed set of deduction tools to the task of finding solutions to the problems in his domain.

The approach to reasoning in a modal logic by reasoning about its semantics may seem counterintuitive at first. Many axioms for defining the semantics of intensional operators tend to be obscure. This obscurity does not make it any easier to arrive at the semantics for an intensional operator. There is no magic method to tell what the "right" possible-worlds semantics for a modal operator is. One must rely on one's intuitions about the commonsense concept that the intensional operator is intended to capture, then decide whether the proposed formal semantics agree with those intuitions in the most critical areas. This criterion renders irrelevant any considerations about whether possible worlds "really exist" in some sense or have psychological reality. Possible-worlds semantics is just a formal tool for modeling certain kinds of inferences drawn by intelligent agents.

The approach that will be adopted is the stating of basic facts about the world in an intensional *object language* that is translated into a first-order *metalanguage*. A set of axiom schemata serves as translation rules that describe the relationship between the two languages. The object language is an intensional language that talks about objects, relations, and actions in the physical world, and about the mental states of agents. The object-language has all the quantifiers and logical connectives of an ordinary first-order theory, except that in the object language such logical connectives as conjunction and disjunction are actually functions that map object-language formulas into other intensional objects. However, the translation is very straightforward because the operators are extensional. For the purpose of expositional clarity, the meaning of the logical operators is intentionally overloaded and the same symbol used in both the object language and the metalanguage. The context will presumably determine the intended meaning, should the distinction be important.

The metalanguage is an extensional language that has as its domain of discourse not only individuals, relations and actions, but also possible worlds and all well-formed expressions in the object language. In addition, the metalanguage has predicates for describing the accessibility relations among possible worlds. Thus, the object language can be regarded as a "high-level" language that is "compiled" into the metalanguage by means of translation axioms that relate the object language to statements in the meta-language about possible worlds. In this book, object language intensional operators will always appear in **boldface** roman type, metalanguage predicates will appear in *UPPERCASE* italic type, and all object language predicates, functions, and constants in Lowercase roman type with an initial capital. Metalanguage variables are in *lowercase* italic type, and schema variables are single uppercase italic letters. Most of the notational conventions and predicate names are taken directly from Moore (1980) to facilitate cross-referencing by the reader.

29

The first task of axiomatizing the semantics of an intensional logic is to devise a formal method for stating that a proposition is true in a possible world. The basic axioms about the semantics of knowledge are the same as described by Moore. A metalanguage predicate, T, which applies to a possible world and an object-language formula, is used to describe this relationship. One possible world is distinguished by virtue of being the current real world, designated W_0. A statement in the object language is true if and only if it is true in W_0. The operator **True** is introduced into the metalanguage to affirm that the object language expression is true in the real world.

$$\mathbf{True}(P) \equiv T(W_0, P)$$

Thus, one way to represent the fact that "Reagan is president" is true would be

$$\mathbf{True}(\text{President}(\text{United-states}) = \text{Reagan})$$

which is equivalent to

$$T(W_0, \text{President}(\text{United-states}) = \text{Reagan}).$$

The next task is to define an accessibility relation on possible worlds that characterizes the semantics of **Know**. We will say that it is true in some possible world w that an agent A knows that a proposition P is true if, for every possible world accessible from w, given the knowledge accessibility relation K for the agent A, P is true in that world. In the metalanguage this is expressed by the following axiom:

(3.1) $\qquad \forall w_1\, T(w_1, \mathbf{Know}(A, P)) \equiv \forall w_2\, K(D(w_1, A), w_1, w_2) \supset T(w_2, P)$

The term $D(w_1, A)$ is the denotation of A in world w_1. Viewed intuitively, this statement means that the only worlds that are possible as far as A is concerned are those that are consistent with what he knows. Since he knows that P is true, P must hold in every possible world consistent with his knowledge. For example, at this moment I do not know whether Ronald Reagan is standing up or sitting down. Therefore the proposition "Reagan is standing" is true in some possible worlds consistent with my knowledge, but false in others. On the other hand, the proposition "Reagan is president" is true in *every* possible world consistent with my knowledge. The relation between possible worlds and a known proposition can be expressed by the diagram in Figure 3.1. In that figure, A knows P because P is true in every world related to W_0 by the accessibility relation K_A. A does not know Q, because Q is true in some accessible worlds and false in others.

The semantics of **Know** requires further elaboration to ensure the possibility of drawing the inferences that could be regarded as intuitively plausible. Since our logic of knowledge is similar to the standard modal logic $S4$, we need some way of capturing Axioms $M3$ and $M4$ in the accessibility relation. The inference that, if a proposition is known, it is true can be drawn by attributing a reflexive

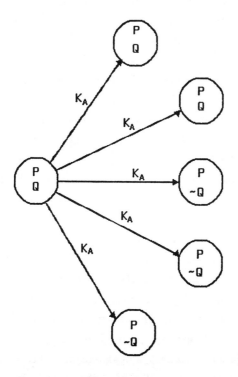

Figure 3.1: *A* knows that *P* is true and *A* does not know whether *Q*

property to the K relation:

$$(3.2) \qquad\qquad \forall a, w \, K(a, w, w).$$

If it is not immediately obvious that reflexivity captures this fact, consider that what the reflexivity property says is that whatever world an agent is in is consistent with the agent's knowledge and that, as a special case, the real world is consistent with any agent's knowledge. In other words, what actually *is* the case is possible according to what one knows. It is not difficult to infer $T(W_0, P)$ from **True(Know**$(A, P))$, and Axioms 3.1 and 3.2. Occasionally an accessibility relation B will be referred to in this book. This is the belief relation, axiomatized like K, except that the axiom analogous to 3.2 is omitted.

It is probably worth pointing out at this time that this formalization of knowledge makes a fairly strong distinction between knowledge and belief. It is impossible to *know* propositions that are not actually true. Of course, no one would dispute the fact that in ordinary discourse we use the English verb "know" in a much broader sense — for example, to indicate a high level of confidence in one's beliefs. It is proper to say something like "I know it will not rain tomorrow." The reason for narrowing our attention to the more restrictive definition of **Know** given here is to avoid the multitude of extremely difficult problems that arise when we attempt to consider beliefs that may not actually be true. We are faced with the problem of representing the fact that beliefs may be held with varying degrees of certainty, and that this variation can and does occur in response to the acquisition of new information. Since changes in the certainty of one belief can exert seemingly arbitrary influence on the certainty of any other belief held by the agent, the problem of maintaining consistency of belief is very difficult. Some work on truth maintainance systems (Doyle, 1979) is relevant to this problem. Belief revision is certainly relevant to utterance planning, because an important factor in planning a declarative statement is whether or not the hearer will believe it. Miscommunication is frequently the result of mistaken beliefs about referring intentions and the discourse context, and an adequate theory of this phenomenon and how agents act to correct it relies on a theory of belief and belief revision. However the research strategy that has been adopted is to consider the simplest cases first, and then later weaken assumptions to cover the more complex realistic cases.

To axiomatize the semantics of a logic like $S4$, Axiom M4 must be captured by the accessibility relation, K. To express this introspective knowledge about knowledge, we follow the course charted so far, i.e., to state that A knows that he knows P is equivalent to stating that $\mathbf{Know}(A, P)$ is true in all worlds consistent with what A knows in the real world. This means that P is true in every world consistent with every world that is consistent with A's knowledge in the real world. This situation of knowing what one knows, which is essentially one of transitivity of the K relation, is expressed in Figure 3.2 and in the following axiom:

$$(3.3) \qquad \forall a, w_1, w_2, w_3 \; K(a, w_1, w_2) \supset [K(a, w_2, w_3) \supset K(a, w_1, w_3)].$$

The relationship among possible worlds shown in Figure 3.2 is similar to the relationship between possible worlds induced by nesting assertions about the knowledge agents have about what other agents know. This relationship can be illuminated by examining Figure 3.3, showing the relationship between the possible worlds describing the situation of John's knowing that Bill knows whether P is true, but not knowing himself whether P is true. This is a situation that a representation used by an utterance planner must be capable of describing, but that many of the simpler proposed representations do not handle adequately. Such knowledge is needed to plan a question and decide who knows the answer, so the planner will know whom to ask. In Figure 3.3, both P and $\neg P$ are true in possible worlds consistent with John's knowledge, so John does not know whether P. However, in all the worlds consistent with John's knowledge in which P is true, P is true according to Bill's knowledge; furthermore, in all worlds in which $\neg P$ is true, $\neg P$ is true according to Bill's knowledge.

Moving beyond a purely propositional object language requires one to confront the problem of terms, and of describing their denotations in different possible worlds. For example, the term "President(United-states)" can denote Jimmy Carter or Ronald Reagan, depending on which possible world one is talking about. One can then assert that "John knows that the President of the United States likes jelly beans," without making any claims that John knows who the President is.

The effect of having an intensional object language is that one must reason explicitly about the denotation of an object language term in the metalanguage for each term that can have multiple denotations. There are some object language terms, called rigid designators, that have the same denotation in every possible world. These terms are treated specially by the system and play an important role in reasoning about whether an agent knows who or what something is. The details of this process are covered in the following section.

Since one must reason about the denotation of terms, a function D is introduced that maps an object language term and a possible world into the denotation

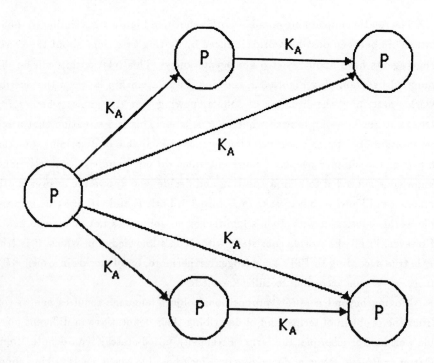

Figure 3.2: If A knows P, then he knows that he knows P.

of that term in the given world. Thus, we might assert

$$D(W_1, \text{President}(\text{United-states})) = D(W_2, \text{Governor}(\text{California})).$$

to state that there was some situation in which the description "President of the United States" denoted the same individual that the description "Governor of California" denoted in some different situation. A metalanguage axiom schema is required to express the fact that two object language terms are equal with respect to a possible world if and only if their denotations are the same in that world:

(3.4) $$\forall w \, T(w, X = Y) \equiv [D(w, X) = D(w, Y)].$$

The introduction of quantifiers into the object language poses a few minor

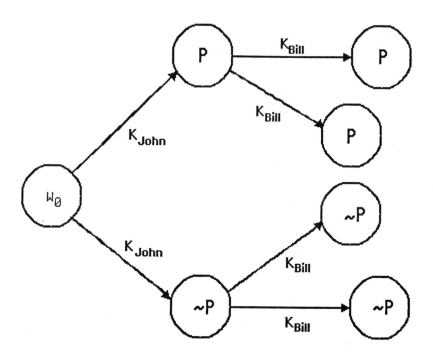

Figure 3.3: John knows Bill knows whether P, but John does not know whether P.

problems arising from the introduction of an object language variable into a term that could have different values in different possible worlds. This problem is referred to in philosophical literature as the problem of "quantifying in," (Kaplan, 1969). In an extensional language, any term that denotes the individual would suffice. However, since the object language is intensional and the terms can have different denotations with respect to different worlds, we have to take into account whether the term substituted for the quantified variable will be evaluated with respect to a different possible world, in which it could denote a different individual.

This difficulty can be circumvented by always substituting a term that has the same denotation in all possible worlds or in other words, a rigid designator. We introduce a function, @, that maps a metalanguage term into an object language rigid designator that has the same denotation as does the metalanguage term in all possible worlds. Thus, the translations of the object language existential and universal quantifiers into the metalanguage are done according to the following two axiom schemata:

$$(3.5) \qquad \forall w \ [T(w, \exists x \, P) \equiv \exists x \, T(w, P[@(x)/x])] \,.$$

and

$$(3.6) \qquad \forall w \ [T(w, \forall x \, P) \equiv \forall x \, T(w, P[@(x)/x])] \,.$$

$P[@(x)/x]$ means that $@(x)$ is substituted for x in the term P wherever it occurs. Because the @ function always constructs rigid designators, the following axiom always holds:

$$(3.7) \qquad \forall w, x \, D(w, @(x)) = x.$$

3.4   Knowing the denotation of a description

Knowing the denotation of a description is of primary importance in the kind of planning that involves actions another agent is expected to carry out, since the planning agent must decide whether the other agent's knowledge is sufficient to allow formulation and execution of the plan. For example, if an agent is to manipulate a piece of equipment, he must know what the piece of equipment is, what the tools are that he is to use, and where they are located.

In the possible-worlds formalism, an agent knows the referent of an object language term if it denotes the same individual in all possible worlds that are consistent with his knowledge. Expressed formally, this statement is equivalent to the schema

(3.8)
$$\forall w_1 \, T(w_1, \mathbf{Knowref}(A, X)) \equiv$$
$$\forall w_2 \, K(D(w_1, A), w_1, w_2) \supset$$
$$D(w_2, X) = D(w_1, X).$$

One can take a similar approach to representing that someone knows which individual satisfies a certain property or set of properties. For example, to say that John knows who murdered Smith is equivalent to saying that there is some individual in the real world about whom John knows that he murdered Smith. In object language notation this is expressed as

$$\mathbf{True}(\exists x \, \mathbf{Know}(\text{John}, \text{Murdered}(x, \text{Smith}))).$$

This example demonstrates why rigid designators are important for the axiomatization of quantifying into the context of a modal operator. One could imagine non-rigid substitutions for x in the above example that would make the statement trivial; for example, let us define a function MurdererOf(x) with its obvious meaning, then substitute MurdererOf(Smith) for x. Obviously, "Smith's murderer murdered Smith" will be true in all worlds consistent with any agent's knowledge. If the existential quantifier in the above example is translated into the meta-language acording to Rule 3.5, then only a rigid designator or rigid function (a function that maps rigid designators into other rigid designators) can be substituted for x, and nonrigid substitutions like MurdererOf(Smith) are ruled out.

3.5 Representing the relationship between knowledge and action

Moore (1980) has proposed an elegant means of formalizing the relationship between knowledge and action on the basis of the possible-worlds formalism. His

Planning English sentences

idea is to use possible worlds to represent the state of the world resulting from the performance of an action. Thus, in addition to the role possible worlds play in describing the semantics of the intensional operators, they also play a role similar to that of situations in a situation calculus (McCarthy and Hayes, 1969; Kowalski, 1974). Moore defines a metalanguage predicate $R(a, w_1, w_2)$ that is true if and only if w_2 is the world resulting from the performance of action a in world w_1, which gives us a way of stating how different worlds are related by the performance of actions.

It should be noted that the use of possible worlds to represent states requires a different interpretation of possible worlds from that commonly used in model-theoretic semantics. In traditional model-theoretic semantics, possible worlds include a temporal history of events and define the truth of all propositions at each point in time. In Moore's approach, a possible world defines the truth of all propositions at a single instant in time, and reasoning about temporal relationships requires reasoning about sequences of possible worlds.

One of the most important problems that arise in attempts to axiomatize actions of any kind is the *frame problem.* This is the problem of specifying for each action precisely which aspects of the world are changed and which ones remain the same after the performance of an action. Since most actions have a very localized effect on the state of the world, it would be ideal to have a convenient way to state formally those few things that do change and then say "everything else remains the same." Saying that "everything else remains the same" is difficult, since it seems as though one either has to have an extremely large number of axioms or must quantify over predicates. Moore adapted Kowalski's approach to stating frame axioms (Kowalski, 1984) to the possible-worlds formalism. The key idea is to translate object language predicates into metalanguage functions that map individuals into intensional objects that can be said to "hold" or "not hold" in a possible world. This reification enables one to quantify over these intensional objects. It becomes possible (in a limited sense) to have the effect of quantifying over predicates in a first-order theory.

The following schema for the translation of object-language predicates into the

38

meta-language will be adopted:

(3.9) $\quad \forall w, x_1, \ldots, x_n \, T(w, P(x_1, \ldots, x_n)) \equiv H(w, :P(D(w, x_1), \ldots, D(w, x_n)))$.

$:P$ is a metalanguage function that maps an individual into an object that holds in a world just in the case that the corresponding predicate P is true of the individual in that world. (Note that the correspondence between functions in the metalanguage and predicates in the object language can be chosen arbitrarily — all that is needed is some simple way of knowing what predicate corresponds to what function. For this purpose, Moore adopted the ":" notation.)

Object language functions and constants are treated analogously. An object language function translates into an intensional object (like the intensional objects corresponding to predicates) that denotes a different individual in each possible world. A function V is defined that maps a possible world and one of these intensional objects into the corresponding individual. Thus, the analogous axiom schema for the translation of object language functions into the metalanguage is

(3.10) $\quad \forall w, x_1, \ldots, x_n \, D(w, F(x_1, \ldots, x_n)) = V(w, :F(D(w, x_1), \ldots, D(w, x_n)))$.

We now have a formal tool for stating frame axioms. The statement that "everything true in w_1 is also true in w_2" can be expressed as

$$\forall p \, H(w_1, p) \supset H(w_2, p)$$

and the statement that "all functions and constants have the same value in w_1 and w_2" is

$$\forall c \, V(w_1, c) = V(w_2, c).$$

One may ask why it is not possible to quantify directly over object language terms in stating frame axioms, since in the metalanguage, one can talk about terms in the object language. The problem is that it then becomes difficult to deal with more complicated assertions involving quantifying-in. For example, suppose one wanted to say that, after an action mapping W_1 into W_2, P is true of everything in W_2 that it was true for in W_1. This would lead us to state a frame axiom that after suitable application of Rule 3.6 is

$$\forall x \, T(W_1, P(@(x))) \supset T(W_2, P(@(x))).$$

39

If we wanted to prove $T(W_2, P(A))$, it would be impossible to use the above axiom, because A does not unify with $@(x)$. What is needed is some way of reasoning about the denotations of all the terms that comprise the object language expression. After using the translation Rules 3.9 and 3.10, we can use Rule 3.7 to reason about the denotation of $@(x)$. The frame axiom becomes

$$\forall x \, H(W_1, :P(x)) \supset H(W_2, :P(x)),$$

and the goal to be proved is

$$H(W_2, :P(V(W_2, :A))),$$

which unifies with the consequent clause of the frame axiom.

With the basic tools for stating frame axioms available, we can now describe how the performance of an action affects the knowledge of various agents. Moore stated axioms for describing the effects of an action on the agent performing the act; however, for utterance planning, several additional situations must be considered. When planning an utterance, a speaker is always dealing with at least one other agent. If one agent performs an action of which the other is unaware, the agent performing the action must be able to reason that the ignorant agent still believes what he believed before the action took place. Furthermore, two agents may be mutually aware of a given action, even though only one of them is actually performing it. In such a case, we want to state how the action affects mutual knowledge. Similarly, one agent, A_1, may perform an action that is observed by a second agent, A_2, without A_1's knowing that A_2 is observing and can see what is going on. Finally, there are actions such as speech acts that always involve at least two agents, with both of them mutually aware of the performance of the action. This section describes the fundamental case of the effect of an action on the private knowledge of an agent. The effect of actions on mutual knowledge will be discussed in Section 5 (of this chapter) which deals with the representation of mutual knowledge. The axiomatization of multiagent speech acts is described in Chapter 5.

To adequately describe the effects of an action on an agent's knowledge requires describing a relationship between two sets of possible worlds — namely, the set of possible worlds consistent with his knowledge before performing the action, and the set of possible worlds consistent with his knowledge after performing the action. If an agent knows about an action in the sense of knowing all of its preconditions and effects, this relationship can be stated by saying that, if w_1 and w_2 are related by event E occurring in w_1, then the worlds consistent with what A knows in w_2 are exactly those worlds that are the result of E's happening in some world that is consistent with what A knows in w_1. This relationship, which is expressed in Figure 3.4, tells us exactly how what A knows after E happens depends on what A knew before E happened.

Figure 3.4 expresses that what is possible according to A's knowledge after performing an action is always the result of performing the action in some world that was possible according to his knowledge before performing the action.

In Figure 3.4, note that it is not the case that there is a world consistent with A's knowledge in w_1 for *every* world consistent with his knowledge in w_0. After doing the action, the world w'_1, in which $\neg P$ is true, is no longer a possible alternative for A. The reason for this is that it is possible for actions to *generate knowledge* by *restricting* the possible worlds that are consistent with an agent's knowledge after performance of the action. In world w_0, the agent does not know whether P is true, since both P and $\neg P$ are true in possible worlds that are consistent with his knowledge. However, after performing a knowledge-producing action, only worlds in which P is true are possible (as far as he knows) in w_1. In other words, the performance of the action has "informed" the agent that P is true.

A meta-language predicate, $R(e, w_1, w_2)$ is introduced to represent that worlds w_1 and w_2 are related by the occurance of event e in w_1, resulting in w_2.

The principles involved here can best be illustrated by a simple example. Suppose we wish to axiomatize the action of removing one part from another in a disassembly operation — $\mathrm{Do}(A, \mathrm{Remove}(x, y))$. The preconditions of this action are that, in the initial state, x must be attached to y, and A must be at the location of y. In the resulting state, x is no longer attached to y; everything else, however, stays the same as in the initial state.

The preconditions are expressed by a set of assertions about what must have been the case in the initial state when it is asserted that an action was performed. Thus, the preconditions can be stated in the following axiom:

(3.11) $\forall a, w_1, w_2, x, y\, R(:\!\mathrm{Do}(a, :\!\mathrm{Remove}(x, y)), w_1, w_2) \supset$

$H(w_1, :\!\mathrm{Attached}(x, y)) \wedge [V(w_1, :\!\mathrm{Location}(a)) = V(w_1, :\!\mathrm{Location}(y))]$

Since Axiom 3.11 quantifies over all worlds w_1, note that it is tantamount to asserting that the preconditions of removing are *universally known*. This is because they hold in *all* possible worlds, including all the worlds consistent with any agent's knowledge.

Next we need an axiom that describes the effects of performing the action when the preconditions are satisfied. Such an axiom would look like 3.12:

(3.12) $\forall a, x, y, w_1, w_2\, R(:\!\mathrm{Do}(a, :\!\mathrm{Remove}(x, y)), w_1, w_2) \supset$

$\forall p\, [((p = :\!\mathrm{Attached}(x, y)) \supset \neg H(w_2, p)) \wedge$

$((p \neq :\!\mathrm{Attached}(x, y)) \supset (H(w_1, p) \equiv H(w_2, p)))] \wedge$

$\forall z\, V(w_2, z) = V(w_1, z)$

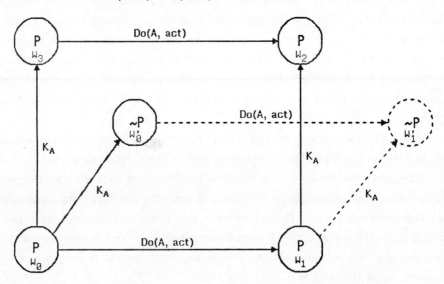

Figure 3.4: The effect of performing an action on the knowledge of the agent

This axiom says three things: (1) the relationship of x being attached to y no longer holds in the world that is the consequence of removing x from y; (2) every other relationship remains unchanged from w_1; (3) the values of all constants and functions (including the denotation of terms) are unaffected by the action.

The final required axioms are ones that relate the agent's knowledge to performance of the action. This is accomplished by asserting that the relationship illustrated in Figure 3.4 holds for the agent performing the action (and possibly also for those agents aware of such performance) and that the knowledge of other agents "stays the same."

(3.13) $\forall a, x, y, w_1, w_2 \, R(:\!\mathrm{Do}(a, :\!\mathrm{Remove}(x,y)), w_1, w_2) \supset$

$\qquad \forall w_3 \, [K(a, w_2, w_3) \supset \exists w_4 \, K(a, w_1, w_4) \wedge R(:\!\mathrm{Do}(a, :\!\mathrm{Remove}(x,y)), w_4, w_3)]$

In essence, what Axiom 3.13 says is that, when an agent performs the removing action, he knows he did it. In other words, every world that is consistent with his knowledge after performing the action is the result of doing the action in some world consistent with his knowledge beforehand. Since we have assumed that the preconditions and effects of removing are universally known to all agents, it is possible, using Axiom 3.13, to prove that the agent must know that the prerequisites held before the action was performed, and that he knows the changes brought about by executing the action and, according to his knowldge, any of their logical consequences.

The axiom

(3.14) $\forall a, x, y, w_1, w_2 \, R(:\!\mathrm{Do}(a, :\!\mathrm{Remove}(x,y)), w_1, w_2) \supset$

$\qquad \forall b, p, w_3 \, [(a \neq b) \wedge B(b, w_2, w_3) \supset \exists w_4 \, K(b, w_1, w_4)]$

$\qquad\qquad [(p \neq :\!\mathrm{Attached}(x,y)) \supset [H(w_3, p) \equiv H(w_4, p)]]$

expresses the fact that all agents other than the one performing the action are "ignorant" of the action or, in other words, after its performance they know precisely what they knew beforehand. They no longer "know" that things that have changed as a result of the action are in their previous state, and, in a more complete axiomatization, one may wish to assert that all of the agents *believe* things are in their previous state. However, because the correct handling of belief involves much more than a slight modification of this axiom, belief will not be considered at this time.

3.6 Representing mutual knowledge

Chapter 5 outlines the necessity for reasoning about mutual knowledge in an utterance planning system. A and B are defined to mutually know P if A knows P, B knows P, A knows that B knows P, B knows that A knows P, A knows that B knows that A knows P, and so on to an arbitrary depth of each agent knowing about the other agent's knowledge. The primary problem encountered in representing mutual knowledge is formulating a finite representation from which a potentially infinite number of facts can be derived. Since one cannot possibly store an infinite number of assertions, one must be able to arrive at some axiom or set of axioms that will allow derivation of the knowledge about knowledge relationships to any arbitrary depth.

Cohen (1978, 1979) proposed a solution to this problem in which sets of assertions about what an agent believes are placed in potentially overlapping spaces in a partitioned semantic network. The set of assertions about a speaker's beliefs is placed on a space labeled SB. The assertions concerning the speaker's beliefs about the hearer's beliefs are placed on a space SBHB, nested within SB. The speaker's beliefs about the hearer's beliefs about the speaker's beliefs are placed in a space inside SBHB called SBHBSB. Mutual belief is represented by a circular link from SBHBSB to SBHB. Thus, SBHB also represents SBHBSBHB, and so on. Derivation of the mutual-belief assertions can then be carried out to an arbitrary depth by following the circular pointers.

Although a scheme similar to Cohen's might work, since there are independent justifications for choosing the possible-worlds semantics approach, we need a means of representing mutual knowledge that fits well within the possible-worlds framework. A special case of mutual knowledge has already been mentioned in the preceeding section, namely, the case in which all agents universally know a certain fact. This can sometimes be accomplished by asserting that the fact is necessarily true. A consequence of necessary truths is that they are true in every possible world consistent with any arbitrary agent's knowledge, and are therefore mutually known by every set of agents. The necessary-truth approach is useful only in stating universal knowledge about things that are immutable, such as the preconditions and effects of an action.

This means of talking about mutual knowledge as necessary truth will not work in all cases. Some things that one would wish to affirm as being universally known are, in fact, not necessarily true in most reasonable models of the world. For example, one may want to assert that it is universally known that the White House is white, but it is not *necessarily* so, since it is logically possible for it to have been pink. This approach also fails when one wants to consider the common case of three agents A, B and C, whereby A and B mutually know P, but C does not.

An approach to representing mutual knowledge that is consistent with the approach outlined so far is a variation of McCarthy and Sato's "any fool" approach (McCarthy et al., 1978). Universal knowledge was axiomatized in solving the *Three Wise Men* problem by hypothesizing an individual called "any fool" and asserting that universal knowledge consists of those facts that "any fool knows." The ability to deal with some types of universal knowledge as necessary truth eliminates much of the need for any individual analogous to "any fool". However, a good solution to the mutual knowledge problem can be found by talking about hypothetical agents that play the role of "any fool" with respect to sets of two or more agents.

The hypothetical "any fool" individual will be replaced by a function that constructs such hypothetical individuals from a list of agents. In this example, I will consider only the case of describing the mutual knowledge of two individuals, A and B. The function that constructs hypothetical agents is called the *Kernel* function, since it is intended to represent the kernel of knowledge that is shared by A and B. The facts that are mutually known by x and y are precisely those facts that are known by the kernel of x and y. The function Kernel(x, y) maps two individuals onto their kernel. Since the argument list of Kernel is unordered, the following axiom is needed:

(3.15) $$\forall x, y \; \text{Kernel}(x, y) \; = \; \text{Kernel}(y, x).$$

What is needed now is a possible-worlds interpretation of the knowledge of Kernel(x, y). The interpretation that immediately suggests itself is to say that the set of possible worlds that are consistent with an agent x is a subset of the possible worlds consistent with the kernel of x and any other agent. This gives us Axiom 3.16:

$$(3.16) \qquad \forall x, w_1, w_2 \, K(x, w_1, w_2) \supset \forall y \, K(\,\text{Kernel}(x, y), w_1, w_2).$$

It should be noted that saying that the worlds consistent with the kernel are a *superset* of the worlds consistent with the agent means that the kernel's knowledge is a *subset* of the agent's knowledge, because the more restrictions are placed on the worlds consistent with an agent's knowledge, the more the agent knows. The two Axioms 3.15 and 3.16 suffice to extend the formalism to handle mutual knowledge between sets of two agents. Figure 3.5 illustrates the relationship among possible worlds that are consistent with the mutual knowledge of two agents.

The solid lines in Figure 3.5 relate those worlds that are consistent with the knowledge of the kernel. The diagram shows how different agents can know different facts, with the kernel representing their mutual knowledge.

Additional axioms must be included with those that describe actions so as to state the effect of the latter on mutual knowledge. This can be accomplished by an intensional operator that states that an agent is *aware* of an event. For example:

$$(3.17) \qquad \forall w_1 \, T(w_1, \mathbf{Aware}(A, \mathrm{Do}(B, \mathrm{Act}))) \equiv$$
$$\forall w_2 \, R(\text{:Do}(\text{:}B, \text{:Act}), w_1, w_2) \supset \forall w_3 \, [K(\text{:}A, w_2, w_3) \supset$$
$$\exists w_4 \, K(\text{:}A, w_1, w_4) \wedge R(\text{:Do}(\text{:}B, \text{:Act}), w_4, w_3)].$$

This axiom says that the effect on knowledge of an agent who is aware of another agent's action is the same as the effect on the agent performing the action, as described in Axiom 3.13 — namely, the agent knows that the action has taken place. Axiom 3.13 says that an agent is aware of his own removal actions, and Axiom 3.17 generalizes this to include other agents as well. If one asserts awareness of the kernel of the two agents, then they are *mutually aware* of the action, and they mutually know that the action has taken place.

3.7   Reasoning about intention

There is a broad spectrum of propositional attitudes that could be categorized under the general heading of "intention." These attitudes include wishes, desires, wants, prior intentions and intentions-in-action, to name a few that have been discussed in the literature (Searle, 1983).

An agent is said to want P if P is not true in the actual world, and there is some set of alternatives to the current world such that each alternative is preferred to the actual world, and P is true in each alternative. An agent may have many of these alternative sets, and may therefore want many propositions. In fact, he may want both P and $\neg P$ under different circumstances, and there is nothing that says that a world in which P is true is even possible to bring about from the current world.

Speech act planning requires a concept of intention that is much narrower than

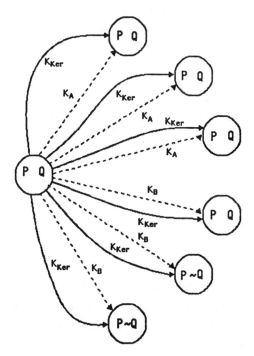

Figure 3.5: A and B mutually know P, A knows Q, B does not know whether Q

wanting. An intention is a want that is distinguished by having been incorporated into an agent's plan. Wants play a causal role in the planning process, but for the time being we will ignore the relationship between wants and intentions, and assume that the speaker's initial intentions are specified as part of the problem to be solved. This view of intention is consistent with what other authors in speech act theory have proposed, however they have frequently used different terminology to refer to the same concept. The role of intention in KAMP is the same as "want" used by Allen, Cohen, and Perrault (Allen and Perrault, 1978; Cohen, 1978), "goal" as used by Konolige (1980), and "prior intention" as used by Searle (1983).

There are two object language intention operators, **Intend** and **Intend-To-Do**. The former applies to an agent and a proposition, the latter to an agent and a term denoting an action. The operators intend to capture those states of affairs in which in the first case, the agent is assumed to have a plan containing a goal to make the proposition true. In the second case, the agent has a plan that contains the intended action.

Ideally, plans should be objects in KAMP's ontology and the definition of intention should refer directly to plans. A complete formal theory of the planning process, which would be required if intention were defined in terms of plans and goals, would be a difficult problem beyond the scope of this investigation. Therefore as an alternative, a possible-worlds semantics for **Intend** has been developed that is similar to the semantics for **Know** and conforms as closely as possible to people's intuitions about the inferences that can be drawn from knowing an agent's intentions, without having to reason directly about plans. The semantics is similar to that of want, described above, since intention is a particular case of wanting.

The semantics of the intention operators differ from the standard modal logic semantics, however, because it is not inconsistent to intend both P and $\neg P$ when both goals are present in the agent's plan. The semantics of **Intend** are that there is a set of possible worlds, s, called an agent's preference set in world w_1, $PS(A, w_1, s)$, such that for every world w in the set s, P is true in w. This is expressed by Axiom 3.18:

(3.18) $\forall w_1\, T(w_1, \mathbf{Intend}(A, P)) \equiv$

$$\exists s\, \mathrm{PS}(A, w_1, s) \wedge \forall w_2\, [(w_2 \in s) \wedge W(A, w_1, w_2)] \supset T(w_2, P),$$

where W is the accessibility relation on possible worlds induced by **Intend** and s is a preference set.

The semantics of **Intend-To-Do** are similar. In this case, there is some preference set s such that, for every world $w \in s$, w is the result of A's performing the action in the current world. This is expressed by Axiom 3.19:

(3.19) $\quad T(w_1, \textbf{Intend-To-Do}(A, act)) \equiv$

$$\exists s\, \mathrm{PS}(A, w_1, s) \wedge$$

$$\forall w_2\, [(w_2 \in s) \wedge W(A, w_1, w_2)] \supset R(\text{:Do}(A, D(w_1, act)), w_1, w_2)$$

It follows directly from 3.18 and 3.19 that, if an agent intends to perform an action, then he intends to bring about its effects. The situation described by these axioms is represented pictorially in Figure 3.6

What is still needed is some sort of distinction between intending and wanting. This distinction comes from an axiom describing restrictions on the worlds belonging to the preference set.

(3.20) $\qquad \forall A, w_1, w_2, s\, \mathrm{PS}(A, w_1, s) \wedge (w_2 \in s) \supset$

$$\exists e, w_3\, K(A, w_3, w_2) \wedge R(\text{:Do}(A, e), w_1, w_3)$$

Axiom 3.20 states that if s is a preference set of A in w_1, and w_2 is any world in that set, then that world must be consistent with what A knows after doing some action. Therefore preference sets do not represent mere desires, but characterize states that are brought about by some actions that A can perform. If e is a subpart of A's current plan, then Axiom 3.20 captures the fact that A intends to bring about the state of affairs characterized by s.

One of the most common inferences the system makes about intention is that, if one agent is helpfully disposed toward another and knows that the other agent intends to bring something about, he then adopts that goal as his own. This relationship, shown in Figure 3.7, establishes one of many possible connections between knowledge and intention.

Viewed intuitively, Figure 3.7 says that, if A knows that some world is consistent with what B intends, then that world is also consistent with what A intends. This is of course a simplified version of what is actually the case. It is seldom true that a person will want everything he knows another person wants. However, if the domain of discourse is restricted to a cooperative endeavor (e.g., the task in a task-oriented dialogue), this assumption will suffice to produce reasonable behavior; it is after all reasonable to assume that the expert and the apprentice will cooperate whenever possible to complete the task. The most obvious situation in a task-oriented dialogue in which this simple approach fails is the one that occurs when the apprentice forms an incorrect plan for carrying out the task, and then wants to achieve goals and perform actions that are not consistent with his inten-

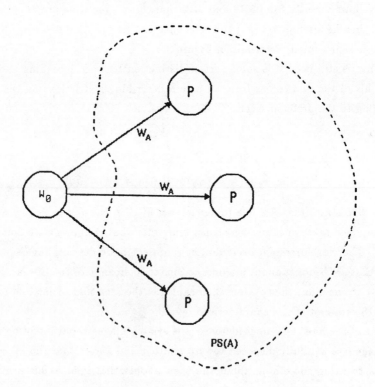

Figure 3.6: The semantics of **Intend**(A, P)

tions. To avoid problems of reasoning about incorrect beliefs, it is also assumed that an agent will formulate a correct plan if he can make any plan at all.

There are several problems with the possible-worlds semantics formalization of intention. One is how to relate the inference rule of necessitation to common-sense intuition. If P is necessarily true, is it reasonable to conclude that every agent intends to bring about P? Certainly agents have not explicitly incorporated the goal P into their plans. However, this assumption does not seem to lead to insurmountable difficulties, because every agent knows that such goals are already achieved in every state of the world.

The most telling difficulty with the possible-worlds formalism is also present with the possible-worlds semantics of **Know**, namely, closure under logical consequence. In the case of **Know**, the logical omniscience assumption could be tolerated because an ideally rational agent performs as though the assumption were valid and, in the domain under consideration, the assumption that an agent could make all possible inferences agreed with our intuition about what was reasonable. However, in the case of **Intend**, the consequential closure assumption is even less agreeable to our intuitions. Agents do not always intend to bring about the logical consequences of their intentions, or even what they *know* to be the

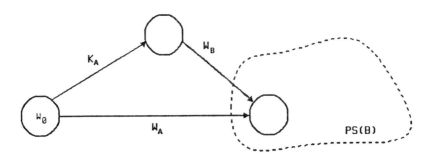

Figure 3.7: One relationship between intending and knowing

logical consequences of their intentions.

Another difficult problem lies in relating an agent's intentions to the actions he performs. The effects of knowledge on an agent who performs an action can be described strictly as a function of the action itself; the agent's prior intentions bear no relevance to any description of what happens to an agent's knowledge when he performs an action. In contrast, the effects of performing an action on an agent's intentions are much more difficult to describe. An action may produce knowledge that in turn affects what the agent intends to do. Even more difficult to describe is how the actions intended by an agent depend on how they fit into his overall plan. For example, if an agent has a plan of doing action A_1 followed by A_2, then, in the initial state of the world, it is reasonable to say that the agent intends to do A_1. After the agent has done A_1, he no longer intends to do A_1, but still intends to do A_2. The change in the agent's intentions is caused not directly by any property of the actions performed by him, but rather by a change in the state of the agent's plan as a result of its partial execution. Therefore, a fully adequate treatment of wanting and intention must entail an adequate logical representation of what it means for an agent to have a plan and to execute a portion of it. The effects on an agent's intentions would be described as the effects of the "metaaction" of executing a step in a plan. A full discussion of the problems involved and their possible solutions is beyond the scope of this work. Some work on metaplanning (e.g., Wilensky, 1980) may be relevant to the problem of reasoning about how intentions change as a result of partial execution of a plan, since, in such a formalization, planning (or executing a step in a plan) can be viewed as an action that exerts its own effects, possibly thereby changing the intentions of the planning agent.

The implicit assumptions made by the system that will enable it to function without the complex machinery of a comprehensive ability to reason about wanting and intention are (1) that all actions are universally known, and (2) that a single plan may be shared by two or more agents.

The first assumption means that the preconditions and effects of all actions are known to all agents, and that all agents know how to perform all actions. This assumption is not as restrictive as it sounds at first. For example, this assumption means that all agents know what it means to remove *part1* from *part2*, in the sense that they know that the action entails locating all the fasteners that connect *part1* to *part2*, locating the proper tool for each fastener, and undoing the connection. Under this assumption, there are still many points at which a planner may be blocked by a lack of knowledge. For example, the agent may not know what the fasteners are or where they are located, he may not know what the right tool is for an unfastening operation, and he might not know where the tool is located.

The simplification achieved by this assumption is that the planner is entitled to the premise that all other agents can expand their goals into plans if they possess correct knowledge about the state of the world. Examination of actual expert-apprentice task-oriented dialogues collected as part of the research on the TDUS system (Deutsch (Grosz), 1975) reveals that this premise is usually borne out in practice. The apprentice always knows generally what it means to remove something — but he does not know in all cases how the removal operation is to be accomplished in a particular instance.

If actions can be assumed to be mutually known, the planner can assume that parts of its plans are shareable. If the planner can show that an agent wants to execute a high-level action, then all the actions constituting the expansion of the high-level action can be assumed to be a plan shared between the planner and the other agent. The planner can assume that each agent can make the same plans that it can, using intensional descriptions of objects in the domain. Thus, the problem of deciding at each step whether an agent wants to perform the next action can be eliminated if it is assumed that the plan is shared. Reasoning about the agent's wants need be done only at the top level to establish that he indeed intends to achieve the high-level goal.

3.8 Conclusion

This chapter has developed a formalism that can serve as the basis for an utterance planning system. As with any formalism, it has both desirable features and some inherent limitations. The desirable features include the power to represent and enable one to reason about knowledge. More specifically, for example, this means the ability to affirm that somebody knows the answer to a question without actually stating the answer, to talk about a person's knowing what something is, and knowing about an action. The inherent limitations include the consequential closure of knowledge and intention.

A number of simplifying assumptions have been utilized in this chapter to avoid having to deal with very difficult problems that are related only tangentially to this research. It is important to realize that the difficulties these assumptions are intended to avoid are not *inherent* limitations of the overall approach. For example, the representation presented here could possibly be extended to nonmonotonic reasoning along the lines of Doyle (1979), to permit a reasonable treatment of belief and belief revision. More sophisticated axioms and deduction techniques could be applied to reasoning about intention so as to draw conclusions about what an agent will do when faced with conflicting goals. Whether the formalism will actually be adequate to handle these more difficult problems, or whether some other scheme will prove more fruitful, is an interesting question to be settled by future research. For the time being, however, there are some pressing problems in reasoning about natural language for which the approach outlined here provides a reasonable starting point from which to seek solutions. Moreover, this methodology enables the system to reason about utterances and their role in a dialogue in a manner that has hitherto not been attempted by a language generation system.

4.2   Planning systems

Underlying the design of planning systems is a considerable body of theory in artificial intelligence, and it would stray beyond the intended scope of this book to review it all here. This section provides a brief review of the basic concept of a planning system for readers who may be unfamiliar with this body of work.

A planning problem consists of a partial description of the world as it is (the *initial state*), a partial description of the world as one would like it to be (the *goal state*), a set of axioms that describe the actions an agent could conceivably perform, and general commonsense facts about the world (e.g., an object cannot be in two places at the same time). The task for the planning system is to find a sequence of actions that an agent (or a set of agents acting cooperatively) might perform that would result in transforming the world from its initial state into the goal state. The goal state is characterized by a well-formed formula $P_1 \wedge \ldots \wedge P_n$, with the stipulation that each conjunct P_i must be true. All actions have *preconditions* (what must be true before an action can be performed) and *effects* (the changes that result from performing the action). Specifying the effects of an action requires enumerating both what it is that changes and (more problematically) what *does not* change as a result of its performance. We shall assume that states are discrete entities, that all actions are performed by some agent (nothing "just happens"), that states are related by the performance of a single action (i.e., only one thing happens at a time) and that all actions have deterministic effects. The problems involved in weakening these assumptions constitute an active area of research in artificial intelligence, and will not be discussed further in this book.

Most planning systems are based on a strategy of search: the space of action sequences is systematically searched for a sequence that has the desired property of achieving the goal. The most commonly used search strategy is *backward chaining*. If one of the conjuncts of the goal wff is P, the set of possible actions is examined for an action for which one of its effects is to make P true. Then the conjunction of preconditions of the selected action is adopted as a subgoal. Some planning systems use *forward chaining* — choosing an action in the current state whose preconditions are satisfied, and then checking to determine whether the goal has been satisfied in the state resulting from its performance. Planning systems have been developed that combine these two search strategies (Rosenschein, 1981).

Several major problems combine to make planning an interesting and difficult enterprise. The first is the sheer size of the search space in all but the most trivial cases. The size of the search space is n^m where n is the number of possible actions and m is the length of the plan. In nontrivial problems, both n and m can be quite large.

The second problem, the question of *interacting subgoals,* is one that frustrates our basic search strategies. Assume that we have a goal consisting of conjuncts $P \wedge Q$. It is unlikely that we have an action in our repertoire that achieves both P and Q at the same time. Therefore, an obvious strategy is to first achieve P, then Q. Unfortunately, if we're not very careful, we can "unachieve" P in the process of achieving Q. Consider the well-known *register-swapping problem* encountered by every student in his first programming course: given variables with values $X_1 = x_1$ and $X_2 = x_2$ and a destructive assignment operation, find a plan to achieve the state in which $X_1 = x_2$ and $X_2 = x_1$. No matter which conjunct of the goal is chosen first, the problem is insoluble without the introduction of a temporary variable. This situation is sometimes referred to as a "double cross."

Another major problem faced by any planning system is that of resource allocation. Typically, there is a limited set of resources available to a planner for achieving its goals. For example, one could assume the existence of a two-handed robot that can execute block-stacking actions. While it is true that the robot could use only one arm to build a tower of blocks, if it devised such a plan, it would not be making optimal use of the resources available. Thus, given the same goal, a two-handed robot should formulate a different plan from a one-handed robot.

A number of approaches to these problems have been advanced in the literature. One of them in particular, resembling Sacerdoti's NOAH planner (Sacerdoti, 1977), has been adopted by KAMP.

4.3   The NOAH planner

Sacerdoti's NOAH planner adopted one set of techniques for dealing with the problems of a large search space, interacting subgoals, and resource allocation. Other solutions have been proposed, but they will not concern us here.

A plausible idea for reducing the size of the planner's search space is to make a "rough cut" plan first, then refine and debug that plan into its final version. The way to make rough-cut plans is to describe the actions available to the planner as part of an *abstraction hierarchy*. The hierarchy will consist of a number of levels, with each action assigned to one of them. The high-level actions very abstractly describe the activity carried out by the agent, with the consequence of omiting considerable detail in their description. Low-level actions, on the other hand, involve very small, detailed steps. For example, a high-level action that might be performed by a hypothetical robot is "remove part A from part B." Intermediate-level actions might involve grasping tools and loosening bolts. The lowest-level actions would operate the robot's effectors directly.

A planner that uses such an abstraction hierarchy is called a *hierarchical planner*. The planning problem is first solved by using only high-level actions, which is normally easy, because there are not many such actions to be considered and they have relatively few preconditions. Next the high-level actions are treated as subgoals that have to be expanded into their constituent actions at the next lower level of abstraction. This process is easier once the initial high-level plan has been formulated, because the search space has been divided into manageable parts by the high-level plan and hence the amount of search required is reduced. This iterative process is repeated until the entire plan has been stated in terms of the lowest-level actions.

NOAH addressed the problem of interacting subgoals by planning to achieve each subgoal independently and then merging the solutions. The independent subgoals are represented in parallel branches of a data structure called a *procedural network,* illustrated in Figure 4.1. One could think of a conjunctive split as representing two independent actions that can be executed in parallel. However, because we are assuming that only one action occurs at a time, true parallelism is not possible. Instead the branches of the split must be ordered for sequential execution. Since the planner is capable of reasoning about partial orderings of action sequences, it is called a *nonlinear* planner.

The merging of parallel branches of a split is accomplished by a set of procedures called critics. Critics can examine a plan for global interactions and make changes in the plan structure to eliminate harmful interactions. Each critic looks for one particular type of interaction and has a single strategy for dealing with it. An example of the kind of interaction that is detected and corrected by critics is a situation in which the effects of actions on one of two parallel branches of a conjunctive split cause the preconditions for the actions on another branch to no longer hold. For example, if given two parallel tasks of painting a ladder and painting the ceiling, the effect of painting the ladder undoes a precondition for painting the ceiling (having a ladder available); therefore the critic modifies the plan by establishing a linear order for the actions (first paint the ceiling, *then* the ladder) in which all the constraints are satisfied.

Critics enable the expansion of goals to remain local and modular, because the expansion process is relieved of the responsibility of checking for global interactions. Although critics deal with the latter, they can be made simple and modular because of the restricted types of interactions considered by each critic. Also, critics do not plan new actions — they only rearrange those that have already been planned to improve efficiency or eliminate harmful interactions. The result is overall simplification of the planning process.

Not only are critics difficult to characterize formally, but there is not even any available proof that they will actually do the job they were designed for. It

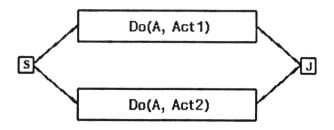

Figure 4.1: A simple conjunctive split

is merely an empirical observation that double-cross situations like the register-swapping problem seem to be relatively rare, and that most problems decompose into subgoals that are quasi-independent — with minimal effort then required to recognize and deal with interactions. Fortunately, the types of interactions that are possible can be characterized systematically and critics developed for the relatively small set they comprise (Sacerdoti, 1977). Therefore, critics are not simply ad hoc procedures that proliferate in response to problems that arise, but rather represent the initial steps toward a theory of the construction and refinement of plans. Reinforcement of this theory by giving it a more solid foundation is an important goal for future research.

NOAH also employed critics for resource allocation. Whenever an action was planned that required that a variable be bound to some existing object, and more than one object could satisfy the binding, the plan was first constructed with dummy bindings called *formal objects* and then critics were invoked to identify the formal objects with actual objects in the domain in a manner that would make the most efficient use of the available resources.

The basic control cycle of NOAH can be described as follows:

1. Goals are expanded at the current level of abstraction.

2. Critics are applied to detect interactions and modify the plan.

3. If the entire plan has been expanded to the lowest-level actions, the process is terminated; otherwise it is repeated and actions on the next lower level of abstraction are considered.

This is also the basic control strategy of the KAMP planner, with certain modifications (outlined in the next section) necessitated by reasoning about knowledge.

4.4   The problems of planning to affect mental states

A planning problem that includes goals and actions involving the mental states of agents is similar in many respects to the traditional blocks-world planning problems that have been studied extensively in artificial intelligence. The world is divided into discrete states, each of which is characterized by a set of logical

60

formulas that describe what is true in that state; in the case of planning to affect knowledge, however, part of this state description includes what the various agents know. Actions are described by functions that map one state into another.

One problem that arises in planning to affect knowledge within *any* formal theory is that of taking into account the fact that agents can reason with their knowledge. If an agent knows that $P \supset Q$ and the planner's goal is to know Q, the planner can proceed by informing him directly that Q is true, or by informing him that P is true and assuming that he can deduce Q to be true. This option is important if the planner is trying to achieve several goals whereby the execution of a single informing action can cause the agent to deduce a number of facts that he needs to know. Such a plan is more efficient than informing him of each fact individually, one at a time.

Konolige and Nilsson (1980) proposed a planning system based on a syntactic representation of agents' knowledge (see Section 3.2). Their planner employed a metalanguage and a reflection principle to encode knowledge of the form $\neg\textbf{Believe}(A, P)$, following Weyhrauch (1980). In such a planning system, actions that affect knowledge are axiomatized as inserting sentences into or retracting them from an agent's belief set. The most serious obstacle raised by this approach is the problem of reasoning efficiently with a reflection principle; it has not yet been possible to resolve this in practice. In spite of its difficulties, this technique is attractive for planning. Since goals are stated in terms of syntactic objects appearing in a belief set, they can be manipulated within a formal theory like physical objects. It is easy to match goals against the effects of actions that produce them — provided, of course, that goals involve only simple logical sentences. However, complex goals involving disjunction that require activation of the reflective machinery would cause trouble for a planning system no matter how it was designed.

The possible-worlds semantics approach to representing knowledge, discussed in Chapter 3, circumvents many of the deduction efficiency problems inherent in the syntactic approach. Unfortunately, planning within this formalism presents problems that have not been faced by previously implemented planning systems.

The ontological assumptions of the possible-worlds approach are quite different from the syntactic approach, a fact that has significant implications for the design of a planning system. Mental states are explicit objects in the syntactic approach because agents are assumed to have goal and belief sets that can be manipulated. In contrast, mental states are not explicit objects in the possible-worlds formalism, but rather are characterized implicitly by the worlds that are consistent with an agent's beliefs or preferences. Achieving a state in which A knows P requires making P true in every world that is consistent with what A knows. The form of this goal is quite different from the goals that previous planning systems have dealt with — goals that consisted of formulas with only existentially quantified variables. A goal involving an agent's knowledge must quantify over all the possible worlds consistent with an agent's knowledge — a potentially infinite set.

4.5 Planning within the possible-worlds formalism

Fortunately, many of the situations in which an agent must plan to tell another agent something are more tightly constrained than the general case; this is because they fall into categories in which good heuristics exist to guide the search for a solution. KAMP solves problems by employing a heuristic problem-solving method that is successful at finding a good plan with minimal effort most of the time while preserving the option of relying on brute-force search if heuristic methods fail.

Problem-solving systems such as STRIPS (Fikes and Nilsson, 1971) have the advantage of employing a simple indexing scheme that can tell what actions are used to achieve particular goals. This is combined with an assumption restricting the predicates used in goals to those that actions are capable of affecting. For example, if there is a goal of the form $On(A, B)$, STRIPS has only to search its index for some action that has an assertion on the add-list that unifies with the goal. It is always obvious from the descriptions of the effects of actions just which of them are potentially useful.

Because of the way actions are axiomatized in the formalism we are adopting, it is impossible to assume that the predicates describing an axiom's effects will always match the predicates that occur in goals; quite frequently the only effect of an action that is stated explicitly will be the assertion of a restriction on a relation between possible worlds and an agent. This is in fact how all illocutionary acts are axiomatized (see Chapter 5). This problem is also complicated by the need to take into account how an agent will reason with his knowledge, which is mentioned in the preceding section. In the possible-worlds formalism, there is no simple indexing mechanism that will connect a desired effect with an action that produces it. Instead, a considerable amount of deduction may be necessary to explicate this relationship.

The fact that this deduction is necessary is a strength as well as a weakness of the formalism. For example, one inference that must be drawn frequently is that, if an agent knows what the effects of an action are and also knows that the action has been performed, then he knows what changes have come about in the world as a result of the action. Allowing the ability to draw this inference means that one does not need two redundant lists of effects for each action, i.e. the effects of the action on the world and the fact that the agent knows each of those effects. In addition to this benefit, the generality of the approach allows one to reason that, if A_1 knows that A_2 performed an action, then A_1 knows what changes occured, even though the axiom never explicitly mentions anything about A_1's knowledge. The generality of this approach does more than simplify the axioms; it extends the system's power to reason about knowledge and action. It is therefore desirable to find some means of retaining the generality while making it possible to plan efficiently.

Many solutions to the problem of determining the effects of actions that are described within the possible-worlds formalism are quite unappealing. One could do a blind forward search, trying all actions to see whether the desired effect could be achieved. However, planning is difficult enough without removing all constraints from the search space. Another solution is to put up with redundancy and axiomatize the knowledge effects of each action individually. The problem goes beyond mere redundancy, however. The effect of a knowledge-producing action such as informing depends on how the new information acquired by the hearer interacts with what the hearer already knows when the action is performed. The problem of specifying in advance *all* the possible consequences of an action seems to be more difficult than the original problem.

The solution adopted by KAMP is to have two descriptions of the actions available to the planner. One is in the form of axioms relating possible worlds, as described in Chapter 3. The axioms describe the actions precisely and in rich detail. The other description is an *action summary,* which summarizes the preconditions and effects of actions in a STRIPS-like formalism using precondition, add and delete lists. The action summaries are used by the planner as a heuristic to guide the selection of actions that are likely to result in a good plan. They are not intended to be complete descriptions of all the consequences of performing the action. The axiomatization is used to reason about whether the proposed plan is going to work. If the action summaries are well designed, the planner will propose correct plans most of the time, and much less searching will be needed to find a correct plan.

The simplifications introduced by the action summaries make it easier to search. For example, an implicit assumption in the action summaries is that all agents know what the effects of the actions are.[1] In some relatively rare instances this assumption may not hold, and any plan proposed that depends on that assumption will fail the verification step. The action summaries are used by a process that can be viewed as a "plausible-move generator," proposing actions that are likely to succeed in achieving the goal.

To illustrate the way action summaries work, consider the example of an action summary for the INFORM action, the axiomatization of which is described in detail in Chapter 3. The action that is being described is more precisely $Do(A, Inform(B, P))$, where A is the agent performing the action (i.e. the speaker), B is the hearer, and P is an object-language proposition that is the object of the INFORM. The axiomatization states that $\mathbf{Know}(A, P)$ and $Location(A) = Location(B)$ are prerequisites, that all agents know this, and the effect when the INFORM is executed successfully is that B and A mutually know that the INFORM has taken place. B can deduce from this knowledge that P is true; therefore, in the resulting state, B knows P. The action summary should provide a simple way of concluding that informing actions are usually a good strategy to employ to get somebody to know something. The action summary would have $\mathbf{Know}(B, P)$ listed explicitly as a knowledge-state effect of the informing action, although the conclusion can be deduced correctly only from the axioms.

64

Prerequisites are also listed as part of the action summary, but there are a number of prerequisites, called *universal preconditions,* that are not listed explicitly because they apply to every action. There are few, if any, preconditions involving the physical state of the world that can be said to apply to every action; however, there are some knowledge-state prerequisites that are both universally applicable and nontrivial. These knowledge preconditions can be summarized by the statement that an agent has to have an executable description of a procedure to do anything. This means that, for each intensional description of any participant in an action, the agent must know the referent of that description. For example, if an agent wants to perform an action like "PointAt(Murderer(Smith))," he must know what "PointAt" means and what individual "Murderer(Smith)" denotes.

In Moore's original treatment of possible-worlds semantics, there was an intensional operator **Can** that was used to capture the notion of universal preconditions. The formula $\mathbf{True}(\mathbf{Can}(\mathrm{Do}(A, X), P))$ means that P is true in the state of the world resulting from A's doing X, and that all the necessary conditions on A's knowledge are satisfied. Since Moore was interested primarily in deducing that a given plan could achieve a particular goal and not in finding the plan in the first place, it was possible to separate the universal preconditions in this manner. In planning, however, the universal preconditions are not really any different from other preconditions. Some may be satisfied in a particular state and others not — and plans must be developed to achieve the latter. Requiring the planner to include the universal preconditions of each action planned captures the generality of Moore's approach while offering enough flexibility for planning.

Action summaries can simplify the process of searching for plans when a significant amount of deduction must be done to find out which action is applicable to accomplish a particular goal. In reasoning about what is true in the states between actions, as when deciding whether or not preconditions have been satisfied, the possible-worlds axioms can be used directly. This approach allows one to have the descriptive power of the possible-worlds knowledge representation while preserving some of the efficiency advantages of simpler approaches.

4.6   Hierarchical planning with KAMP

The planning system described in this chapter is different from planners like STRIPS in which all actions are described on the same level of detail. It has been frequently observed (e.g., Sacerdoti, 1977) that searching such an unstructured space can be quite inefficient. A good strategy for searching such a space is to first construct a high-level plan that ignores some of the preconditions and effects of the actions, then, on a second pass, to consider the more detailed effects and make minor adjustments in the overall plan to accommodate the finer detail. Of course it is not necessarily true that the needed adjustments will be minor. It is not difficult to construct such pathological examples as the register-swapping problem, whereby the interaction of the effects of two actions necessitates complete revision of the plan. It merely seems a reasonable heuristic to apply to problems in many domains, a conclusion supported by experience.

The planning of linguistic actions exemplifies a domain in which hierarchical planning is a good technique to use because the range of available actions is large and the nature of their preconditions and effects is such that they do not usually interfere with each other. This implies that decomposition of conjunctive goals usually works. For example, it is difficult to imagine a situation in which the performance of one speech act makes another one that is part of the same coherent plan impossible. Which action is performed first may influence the realization of the second; however, "double cross" situations like the register-swapping problem occur rarely in regular conversation, if at all.

In utterance planning there are at least two clearly defined levels of abstraction: deciding to perform an illocutionary act such as informing or requesting, and constructing an utterance that will implement the high-level speech acts. In Chapter 6 we will see how these two levels can be subdivided further. Hierarchical planning allows the language production process to be divided into levels of abstraction, while enabling the interaction between levels that is essential for planning utterances. The latter is such a complex process that it is difficult to imagine planning without an abstraction hierarchy of actions to reduce the search space to manageable size.

4.7 KAMP's data structures

KAMP is a hierarchical planner whose basic design is similar to Sacerdoti's NOAH planner described in Section 4.3. The control strategy and data structures employed by the two systems are quite similar, although they differ in relatively minor respects. The underlying representation and deduction systems upon which the two systems are based are radically divergent, with some of the differences also stemming from the problems caused by planning in a multiple agent environment.

The data structure used by KAMP to represent plans is called a *procedural network*. The distinguishing feature of procedural networks is that they allow action-sequencing information to be specified as minimally as possible. Plans can be represented as partially ordered sequences of actions and then a linear ordering of actions need be imposed only when sufficient information has been gathered. This has the advantage that one can avoid committing oneself to an incorrect linear ordering that would subsequently have to be discarded.

A procedural network can be thought of as a two-dimensional data structure. The horizontal dimension is a temporal one reflecting the partial ordering of the actions. The vertical dimension is one of abstraction, along which goals and abstract actions are refined into sequences of low-level executable actions. Figure 4.2 is an example of a simple procedural network.

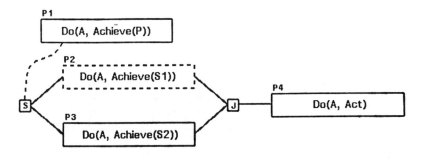

Figure 4.2: A simple procedural network

Goals and actions are represented in the network as PLANSTEP nodes, shown as rectangular boxes in Figure 4.2. KAMP represents both goals and actions in the network. Goals can be thought of as very-high-level actions, with vaguely specified conditions on what is true after the action is perfromed. The planner knows that the goal will be true in the resulting state, but it cannot yet reason about everything that will have changed. Node *P*1 in Figure 4.2 is a PLANSTEP for a high-level goal, while *P*2, *P*3, and *P*4 are low-level expansions of *P*1. *Phantoms* are goals that are already true in the current state of the world, so nothing has to be done to achieve them. They are represented in the diagrams by boxes consisting of dotted lines like *P*2 in Figure 4.2. Phantom goals are kept as part of the plan because subsequent changes in the partial order of the actions may make it necessary to "undo" the effects of a previous action, and thus "unsatisfy" a phantom goal. Actions are represented by PLANSTEP nodes that contain a metalanguage description of the action to be performed. It is possible for high-level actions to be *subsumed,* which means that their principal effects are achieved through minor alterations in the low-level expansion of another action in the plan, rather than by direct expansion to the lower level. Speech acts are often subsumed — a process that is discussed in greater detail in Chapter 6.

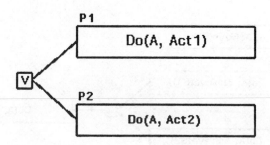

Figure 4.3: A disjunctive split

There are two types of nodes in the plan, which represent alternatives among plan steps. *Choice* nodes split the plan into several parts, depending on which of several alternatives is selected. The goal could be achieved by executing *either* of the branches $P1$ or $P2$ in Figure 4.3. If the expansion of one of the branches of the choice fails, it is pruned from the plan and the other branches are expanded. The *split* nodes implement the partial ordering of plan steps. For the plan to succeed, each branch of a split must eventually be executed, but there is no commitment at that level to the order in which the branches are executed. In KAMP, splits are not intended to represent concurrent actions; the planning formalism described here has difficulty with concurrent actions because of the use of possible worlds as discrete states brought about by the performance of single actions. The split expresses the fact that there is no commitment to ordering the branches of the plan at some stage in the planning process. A linear ordering will eventually be chosen — arbitrarily if no better strategy presents itself — but the decision will be postponed as long as possible.

It is also possible to describe nodes for iterated plan steps and conditional branches, but situations in which these constructs are necessary will not occur in any of the examples to be considered.

The connection between the planning data structure and the possible-worlds-semantics formalism is made by associating with every node of the plan a world that represents the actual state of affairs at each point. Whenever a fact has to be proved to hold in the situation resulting from the execution of a series of actions, this is done by using the world associated with the appropriate node in the procedural net as the current real world.

Figure 4.4 illustrates how worlds are associated with the expansion of a high-level action into low-level actions. The world resulting from the execution of the low-level actions is precisely the same world that results from performing the high-level action. If the frame axioms for the high- and low-level actions are carefully designed, it then becomes possible to specify incrementally what aspects of the world remain the same at each level of abstraction.

For example, let us consider a robot engaged in a block-stacking task involving several blocks on a table. Suppose a high-level action of building a tower is proposed. It is conceivable that the block stacking and unstacking operations required to expand tower building to an executable description may effect a number of changes in the state of the blocks on the table that cannot be predicted at the time the tower-building action is proposed. However, it is reasonable to assume that, no matter what actions are planned as part of that expansion, the position of the furniture in the room will not change. All that can possibly change is the position of blocks on the tabletop. This fact can be incorporated in the statement of a frame axiom for the tower-building action.

Using this formalism, the planner can propose a high-level plan and might be able to work on later parts of it without having to expand the initial parts to complete low-level detail. If a situation arises in which information is required that depends on expansion of an earlier part of the plan, the planner can return to the other part of the plan and expand it further before continuing. The ability to state frame axioms for actions at different levels of abstraction is another advantage of KAMP over other hierarchical planning systems.

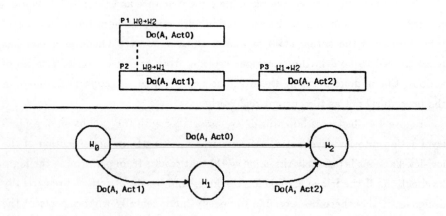

Figure 4.4: Associating worlds with the expansion of an action

4.8 How KAMP formulates a plan

KAMP is a multiagent planning system that forms plans involving cooperative actions among several agents. KAMP's data base contains assertions about what each of the agents knows, and what each knows that the other agents know. KAMP is a "third person" planner because it is not actually one of the agents doing the planning, but is rather able to simulate the planning done by the agents, given certain information about them. When KAMP plans, it "identifies" with one of the agents and makes plans from the perspective of the agent it is identifying with. This perspective makes an important difference when the planner considers the intentions of other agents. If we assume that an agent A_1 doing the planning has a particular goal to achieve, it is possible for the planner to assume that A_1 will intend to perform any action that A_1 knows will contribute to achieving the goal. However, if it is necessary to incorporate the actions of another agent, A_2, into the plan, A_1 must be able to show that A_2 will actually perform the actions required of him. This amounts to showing that A_2 *intends* to carry out the action. Guaranteeing that this condition holds can lead to the planning of requests and commands. Once it is established that A_2 intends to perform a high-level action, the planner thereupon assumes that A_2 will intend to effect any action that he knows will contribute toward the realization of the high-level action. A_2 may not have the knowledge necessary to carry out the action, but it can be assumed that A_2 will execute a plan if he can figure it out.

When the planner is given an initial goal, it starts by creating a procedural network consisting of a single plan step that contains the goal. Then the following process is executed repeatedly until either the planner concludes that the goal is unachievable, or some sequence of executable, (i.e., low-level) actions is found that achieves the goal. First, possible worlds (serving in their role as states of affairs) are assigned to each of the nodes in the procedural net reflecting the actual state of the world at that time (i.e., at the time *before* the action or goal named in the node is performed or achieved). The initial node is assigned W_0, the initial actual world. Then, iteratively, when the planner proposes that a subsequent action be performed in a world to reach a new world, a name is generated for the latter, and an R relation (see Section 3.5) linking the original world, the new world, and the action is asserted in the planner's database. All goal nodes that have worlds assigned to them are then evaluated — i.e., the planner, using the world assigned to that node as the current state of the actual world, calls on the deduction system to attempt to prove that the goal is true. Any goal for which the proof succeeds is marked as a phantom goal.

In the next step, all the unexpanded nodes in the network that have been assigned worlds, and that are not phantoms, are examined. Some of them may be high-level actions for which procedures exist to determine the appropriate expansion. These procedures are invoked; otherwise the node is an unsatisfied goal node, and the action generator is invoked that uses the action summaries to propose a set of prospective actions that might be performed to achieve the goal. If an action is found, it is inserted into the procedural network along with its preconditions, those that are universal as well as those specifically related to the particular action.

The cycle of criticism begins next. Critics play the same role in KAMP as they do in NOAH. Each critic has one type of global interaction that it tests for in the plan, and a single strategy for dealing with this interaction.

After the cycle of criticism has finished, the planner checks to see if all goals and high-level actions have been fully expanded to the next level. If the expansion is complete, the planner invokes the deduction system to prove that the proposed sequence of actions actually achieves the goal. If the proof is successful, the process of world assignment is carried out again and the entire procedure repeated.

If the proof fails, the planner removes the current choice from the plan and checks to see whether other choices can be expanded. The failure of the proof may be due to the inadequacy of the action summaries; if such is the case, the planner has no feasible alternative to a brute force perusal of the search space.

The planner iterates the process of expansion and criticism until the entire plan has been expanded to the current level in the abstraction hierarchy. Next, the entire process is repeated for actions at the next lower level of abstraction. If the planner is already at the lowest level and all critics have been applied to the resulting plan, then a complete, executable plan has been found.

4.9 An example of planning to affect knowledge

The operation of KAMP and its utilization of the knowledge representation on which it is based can perhaps best be understood by means of a simple example. Let us consider the following problem. A robot named Rob and a man named John are in a room that is adjacent to a hallway containing a calendar. Both Rob and John are capable of moving, reading calendars, and talking to each other, and they each know that such capabilities are universal. They both know they are in the room, and they both know where the hallway is located. Neither Rob nor John knows what date it is. Suppose further that John wants to know what day it is, and that Rob knows John's desire. Furthermore, Rob is helpful and wants to do what he can to ensure that John will achieve his goal. We would like to see KAMP devise a plan, perhaps involving actions by both Rob and John, that will result in John's knowing what day it is.

We would like to see Rob devise a plan that consists of a choice between two alternatives. First, if John could find out where the calendar is, he could go to the calendar and read it; in the resulting state, he would know the date. So, Rob might tell John where the calendar is, reasoning that this information would be sufficient for John to form and execute a plan to achieve his goal. The second alternative is for Rob to move into the hall, read the calendar himself, return to the room, and then tell John the date.[2]

This research does not entail a detailed effort to axiomatize temporal knowledge. Currently, KAMP's temporal reasoning is now based on action sequences; it has no sense of the passing of time other than the occurrence of events. To simplify the example, we shall assume no change in the date while the plan to read the calendar is being formulated and executed.

First we need some basic axioms to describe the state of the world and the possible actions. The date is considered to the the denotation of the term "Date." Knowing the date is equivalent to knowing the denotation of Date. It is universally known that the calendar Cal1 tells the date, so we have the axiom

(4.1)   **Necessary**(Date = Info(Cal1)).

where Info(x) is taken to denote whatever information is written on x that can be read by some agent, and **Necessary**(P) means that P is true in all possible worlds. We need some simple axioms stating the basic facts of the problem:

(4.2)   **True**(**Know**(John, Location(Rob) = Loc1))

(4.3)   **True**(**Know**(Rob, Location(John) = Loc1))

(4.4)   **True**(**Know**(Rob, Location(Cal1) = Loc2))

(4.5)   **True**($\neg$**Knowref**(Rob, Date))

(4.6)   **True**(**Know**(Rob, $\neg$**Knowref**(John, Date)))

(4.7)   **True**(**Know**(Rob, $\neg$**Knowref**(John, Location(Cal1))))

(4.8)   **Necessary**($\forall A$ **Knowref**(A, Location(A)))

Three actions can be performed by agents in this domain: moving, informing, and reading. The axiomatization of informing is given in Chapter 5. Reading, axiomatized as follows, is a type of knowledge producing action that does not involve a speech act:

(4.9) $\forall A, x, w_1, w_2 \, R(\text{:Do}(A, \text{:Read}(x)), w_1, w_2) \supset$
$$V(w_1, \text{:Location}(A)) = V(w_1, \text{:Location}(x)).$$

(4.10) $\forall A, x, w_1, w_2 \, R(\text{:Do}(A, \text{:Read}(x)), w_1, w_2) \supset$
$$\forall z V(w_2, z) = V(w_1, z) \wedge \forall p H(w_2, p) \equiv H(w_1, p)$$

(4.11) $\forall A, x, w_1, w_2 \, R(\text{:Do}(A, \text{:Read}(x)), w_1, w_2) \supset$
$$\forall w_3 \Big[K(A, w_2, w_3) \supset$$
$$\exists w_4 \, K(A, w_1, w_4) \wedge R(\text{:Do}(A, \text{:Read}(x)), w_4, w_3) \wedge$$
$$\forall z[z = \text{:Info}(x) \supset V(w_3, z) = V(w_1, z) \wedge$$
$$z \neq \text{:Info}(x) \supset V(w_3, z) = V(w_4, z)] \Big] \wedge$$
$$\forall p \, H(w_3, p) \equiv H(w_4, p).$$

Axioms 4.9, 4.10, and 4.11 look complicated, but it is not difficult to see what they say if one bears the following facts in mind. Axiom 4.9 states the precondition that, if an agent is reading something, he must be in the same place as the object he is reading. Axiom 4.10 describes the physical effects of reading, which are null. The axiom says that, after an agent has read something, anything that was true of the world before will also be true afterwards, and the values of all functions and constants remain unchanged. Axiom 4.11 describes the really important effect of reading — namely, that after he has read something, an agent knows the value of the expression written on the object.[3]

Moving can be thought of as a strictly physical action whose only knowledge effect is that the agent knows he has just moved. The axiomatization of the action $\mathrm{Do}(A, \mathrm{Move}(x, y))$ is reasonably straightforward and will not be described in detail here. All predicates stay the same and all terms except the one describing the location of the agent retain the same value. The only precondition is that the agent's starting location is in the initial location x.

For each action, it is necessary to define an action summary. The following are summaries for the actions used in this problem:

Action:	$\mathrm{Do}(A, \mathrm{Inform}(B, P))$
Preconditions:	**True**$(\mathrm{Location}(A) = \mathrm{Location}(B))$
	True$(\mathbf{Know}(A, P))$
K-Effects:	**True**$(\mathbf{Know}(B, P))$
P-Effects:	None
Action:	$\mathrm{Do}(A, \mathrm{Informref}(B, P))$
Preconditions:	**True**$(\mathrm{Location}(A) = \mathrm{location}(B))$
	True$(\mathbf{Knowref}(A, P))$
K-Effects:	**True**$(\mathbf{Knowref}(B, P))$
P-Effects:	None
Action:	$\mathrm{Do}(A, \mathrm{Read}(X))$
Preconditions:	**True**$(\mathrm{Location}(A) = \mathrm{Location}(X))$
K-Effects:	**True**$(\mathbf{Knowref}(A, \mathrm{Info}(X)))$
P-Effects:	None

Action:	$\text{Do}(A, \text{Move}(X, Y))$
Preconditions:	**True**$(\text{Location}(A) = X)$
K-Effects:	None
P-Effects:	**True**$(\text{Location}(A) = Y)$

For the sake of simplicity, we will assume that "John", "Rob", "Call", "Locl" and "Loc2" are rigid designators.

KAMP is given the goal **Knowref**(John, Date) and is instructed to plan from the perspective of the individual Rob using world W_0 as the initial state of affairs. The planner creates a single-node procedural network consisting of the given goal.

KAMP first attempts to show that the agent doing the planning (in this case Rob) knows whether the goal is satisfied. If he does not know, he has to formulate some sort of plan to find out. To simplify the problem, we assume that Rob already knows that John does not know what date it is (perhaps John just asked Rob for the date) so KAMP does not need to work on this "metagoal."

KAMP then searches the plan for any high-level actions that need to be expanded and for any unexpanded goal nodes. When a goal node is found, and the action summary list is consulted for actions that include some knowledge-state effect that matches

Knowref(Rob, Date).

The goal matches the knowledge effects of two actions: Informref and Read. The planner knows that John will know what date it is if somebody informs him, or if he finds something he can read that will tell him the date. Since, in our simple axiomatization, knowing the date is equivalent to knowing what Call says, and since Rob is the only other potential informing agent in our environment, the plan becomes a choice between either Rob's telling John the date, or John's reading Call.

KAMP creates a choice node to represent the disjunction of these two alternatives and adds the specification that each precondition of the action (including the universal preconditions) be fulfilled, thus resulting in the procedural network of Figure 4.5.

KAMP works on expanding each branch of the choice in turn. The first branch consists of Rob's telling John what date it is. The preconditions for this informing action are that Rob should be in the same place as John and that Rob should know what information he is to convey, i.e., he has to know himself what date it is.[4] In a manner similar to the previous step, KAMP attempts to show first that

$$\mathbf{Know}(\mathrm{Rob}, \mathrm{Location}(\mathrm{Rob}) = \mathrm{Location}(\mathrm{John}))$$

which follows from Axiom 4.2 that Rob is in the room (Loc1), from Axiom 4.3 that Rob knows John is in the room, and from Axiom 4.8 which says in general that everyone always knows where he is. KAMP cannot show that Rob knows what date it is, because it is asserted as part of the problem that he does not — and so a new subgoal is created to achieve a state in which Rob knows what date it is.

Expanding the goal **Knowref**(Rob, Date) is done by a process similar to the expansion of **Knowref**(John, Date). The action summaries are consulted and KAMP discovers that Rob will know the date if either somebody tells him or he reads the calendar. Since there is only one other agent in our environment, if anyone tells Rob what day it is, it would have to be John. However, this leads to the precondition **Knowref**(John, Date) which is already part of the plan we are trying to accomplish. KAMP, recognizing this circularity, will not propose that John inform Rob of the date.

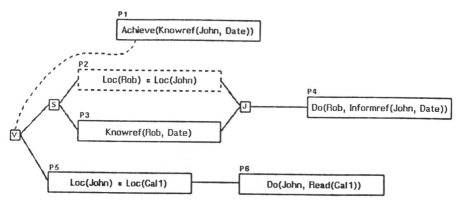

Figure 4.5: Rob tells John the date, or John reads the calendar

Consequently, the only action resulting from the expansion of **Knowref**(Rob, Date) is that Rob reads Call. To do this, Rob must be in the same location as Call, and all the universal preconditions must be satisfied. In this case, all that means is that Rob must know what Call is, and that is satisfied because Call is a rigid designator. The expansion results in the procedural net shown in Figure 4.6

The next cycle of expansion finds the goal of Rob's being at the calendar, a goal that is unattained in the current state of the world because Rob is in the room with John. The action summaries give moving as the necessary action to get Rob to a different location, so KAMP plans for Rob to move from Loc1 to Loc2. In the action summary, Loc2 is described intensionally as the location of the thing being read or, in this case, Location(Call). The planner must then establish the universal precondition for this action, namely, that Rob knows the denotation of the term Location(Call). This fact is provided as part of the specification of the problem in Axiom 4.4.

At this point there are no more goal nodes generated, so in a sense we have a complete plan — it has been expanded down to the lowest level of detail. The plan, however, is incomplete; if one were to attempt to prove it correct, one would fail. The problem is that, once Rob moves out into the hall to read the calendar,

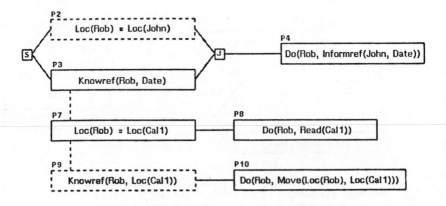

Figure 4.6: Rob must be at the calendar and must read the calendar

he can no longer inform John of the date because John is back in the room where Rob left him.

Not much has been said about plan criticism up to this point because, until this point in the plan, no critics were applicable. After each cycle of expansion is finished, the critic procedures are invoked. Each critic looks for a specific condition in the plan and, if the condition obtains, makes modifications in the plan that, it is hoped, will result in some sort of improvement, either in correctness or efficiency.

In this case, there is a critic procedure called *ResolveConflicts* that looks for split nodes for which all the goal nodes have been expanded on at least one branch of the split. *ResolveConflicts* looks at all the other goal nodes on other branches of the split to see whether they are still satisfied after execution of the expanded branch. If not, an ordering is imposed on the split so that the goal is achieved *after* the expanded branch has been executed. KAMP assumes that some such ordering will eventually work.

In this case, KAMP removes the phantom designation from the goal labeled *G2* in Figure 4.5, and places the goal after the sequence of actions it has just determined (see Figure 4.7).

Achieving the goal "Location(Rob) = Location(John)" is the same as achiev-

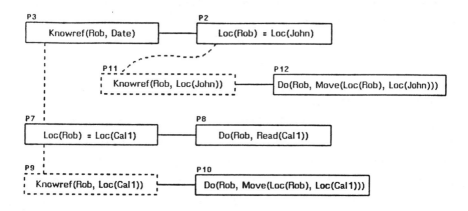

Figure 4.7: After criticism by the resolve-conflicts critic

ing the other location goal, and a move action is planned to get Rob back into the room with John before Rob carries out the informing action.

At this point, the plan has been completely expanded and no more critics apply, so KAMP tries to verify that it is correct. In this case the plan can be verified, so no further work is needed.

As the expansion of the other alternative to the top-level choice is similar, it will not be described in detail. KAMP plans for John to move to the location of the calendar and read it; in the resulting state John will know the date. Using the universal preconditions, KAMP reasons that for John to move to the calendar, he must know where it is. One way he can find this out is for Rob to tell him, so KAMP incorporates an informing action into Rob's plan to accomplish this subgoal.

4.10   Why implement a planning system?

Much of the knowledge used by KAMP in the course of planning is distributed throughout the system in different ways. Some is found in the action summaries, some is found in the procedures that expand high level actions to lower abstraction levels, and some is procedurally embedded in critics. The criticism that one can direct toward a system organized in such a fashion is that it is ad hoc. It is very easy to write a few lines of code (called "procedural knowledge" for the sake of respectability) to perform admirably on a limited class of examples, while lacking any capability of generalization to a wider class of problems. All too frequently in the field of artificial intelligence, such systems are offered as theories that purport to explain some cognitive process, while they really explain nothing at all because of their limited generality.

As a theory of the relationship between a speaker's communicative intentions and the utterances he produces, KAMP is not subject to this criticism, because while knowledge about the language generation process is distributed throughout action summaries and various procedures, everything the planner does must ultimately be justified by the axioms. The step of plan verification discussed in Section 4.5 is not only important for informing the planner when its heuristics have led it astray, but it is also important from the standpoint of the implementor because it guarantees that the methods of implementation are consistent with the theory.

Therefore, KAMP's theory of communication is embodied strictly in the axioms describing the relationship between different levels of linguistic actions and their effects on the speaker's and hearer's knowledge. While these axioms may not be an adequate account of this complex process, they do provide a testable theory. One can examine a dialogue and ask the question "Does the observed behavior follow from a reasonable set of assumptions and the axioms of communication?" If the answer is "no," then the investigation of why this is so is likely to lead to an improved theory.

One may then be led to ask the question, "If the real theory on which KAMP is based is embodied only in the axioms, why not simply list the axioms describing the communication process, and forget about the implementation of the planner altogether?" The answer is that the process that operates according to the theory is of interest as well. An example of an important processing issue addressed by KAMP is whether a language generation process should be modularized into "what to say" and "how to say it" components — a matter about which the axioms have nothing to say.

The KAMP implementation can be regarded as a theory, not about communication or language generation, but rather about how a process that must draw upon the various knowledge sources that come into play during utterance planning is best organized. Naturally, the implementor of such a system must address many issues associated with how the knowledge expressed by the axioms can best be brought into play during the planning process. If any performance at all is to be achieved, then all of these implementation problems must be solved at some level, even if that implies that some ad hoc solutions will be adopted. Therefore, there are some things that KAMP does well, and there are others that are ad hoc. However, the goal of future research on utterance planning systems is to replace the ad hoc components with those that rely on more general principles.

KAMP, therefore, embodies two theories: a theory of the process of planning communication, and of communication itself. Both of these theories are necessary to develop and extend our understanding of linguistic behavior, and each theory places demands and constraints on the other. It is for this reason that the implementation of KAMP is an important part of this research enterprise.

4.11   Conclusion

This chapter has discussed several problems in planning to affect the mental state of agents. Chapter 3 discussed the problems of representing and reasoning about what agents want and believe. It would be desirable for a planning system to make use of the possible-worlds formalism for reasoning about how to influence an agent's knowledge. Because planning to affect an agent's knowledge requires reasoning about what he can deduce when some new information is added to his knowledge, it is generally difficult to determine in advance exactly how a given action will affect what he knows. To reduce the amount of search needed to find a correct plan, action summaries are used to describe common, stereotypical effects of actions on knowledge and the physical world. The planner can use these general heuristics to find a plan that can then be verified in an actual situation.

This chapter has introduced the subject of planning by an agent to affect some other agent's knowledge. Chapter 5 considers the planning of illocutionary acts in greater detail, while Chapter 6 deals with the problem of producing utterances and the way this process interacts with the high-level planning procedures described herein.

5

Planning illocutionary acts

5.1 What is a speech act?

Speech act theory has its roots in the work of Wittgenstein, who in *Philosophical Investigations* proposed an analogy between using language and playing games. His basic point was that language is a form of rule-governed behavior, much the same as game-playing, employing rules and conventions that are mutually known to all the participants.

The field of speech act theory is usually considered to have been founded by Austin (1962) who analyzed certain utterances called performatives. He observed that some utterances do more than express something that is true about the world. In uttering a sentence like "I promise to take out the garbage," the speaker is not saying anything about the world, but is rather undertaking an obligation. An utterance like "I now pronounce you man and wife" not only does not say anything that is true about the world, but when uttered in an appropriate context by an appropriate speaker, actually *changes* the state of the world. Austin argued that an account of performative utterances required an extension of traditional truth-theoretic semantics.

The most significant contribution to speech act theory has been made by philosopher John Searle (1969, 1979a, 1979b), who was the first to develop an extensive formulation of the theory of speech acts. The theory can be summarized as follows. Utterances are actions called *illocutionary acts.* These fall into several general categories such as *directives,* (request, command, etc.), *representatives,* (inform, lie, etc.), *commissives,* (promise, threaten, etc.) *expressives,* (apologize, thank, etc.) and *declarations* (utterances that change the state of the world).

There are other levels of abstraction at which an utterance can be viewed — for example, as a series of *utterance acts,* i.e., speaking a series of phonemes, or as *propositional acts,* which include such actions as referring. Searle analyzed these different categories of speech acts and proposed semiformal sets of conditions under which they might be successfully performed. For example, for each illocutionary act there would be physical enabling conditions as well as conditions on those beliefs and intentions of the speaker that must be satisfied, if the action is to be carried out sincerely and effectively.

Viewed on the intentional level, utterances have two primary components: *illocutionary force* and *propositional content.*[5] Sentences typically have some means of indicating what speech act the speaker is performing (called an *illocutionary-force indicator*) as well as expressing a propositional content. For example, performative utterances possess explicit illocutionary force indicators in the form of illocutionary verbs as in the sentence, "I hereby order you to take out the garbage." However, it is much more common to rely upon the syntactic form of the utterance to give a clue as to its illocutionary force; for example, imperative utterances are frequently used to issue commands ("Take out the garbage!"). Finally, there are *indirect speech acts* in which the syntactic form of the utterance does not correspond directly to the speaker's intended illocutionary force. An example is "Do you think you could take out the garbage?" in which the speaker intends his question to be understood as a request to take out the garbage.

The effect of performing an illocutionary act successfully is that the hearer thereby acquires some knowledge of the speaker's intentions. For example, if a speaker S informs a hearer H that P by producing an utterance U, then the effect of this action is that H knows that S intended to inform H that P and furthermore, intended that this recognition be accomplished by virtue of H's knowledge of the meaning of U. Of course, a speaker may have intentions that go beyond the immediate illocutionary effect; for example, his aim may be to have H actually believe P or, perhaps, to make H angry. Such effects are referred to as *perlocutionary effects* and are the primary reasons for planning speech acts. However, the realization of perlocutionary effects is really under the control of the hearer rather than the speaker, so there is nothing a speaker can do to *guarantee* that his intended perlocutionary effects will be attained. He can only reason on the basis of his beliefs about the hearer that a correctly performed illocutionary act will result in the intended perlocutionary effects. Modeling the process that leads from illocutionary to perlocutionary effects complicates the axiomatization of speech acts and is one of the factors that make the planning of speech acts a nontrivial problem.

Unlike illocutionary intentions, perlocutionary intentions need neither be recognized nor intended to be recognized. In some cases (such as intentionally flattering someone) the goal is that the hearer *not* recognize the perlocutionary intention, but merely be put into the right mental state.

The term "speech act" is often imprecise because it is not clear what level of abstraction is being addressed. What a speaker is doing when he says something depends on the level at which the communicative act is described. Figure 1.5 illustrates the different levels when such actions are described.

At the level of utterance acts, the speech act is viewed as a mere physical phenomenon. The speaker has just uttered a sequence of words, nothing more. A speaker concerned only with this level of description might say "Testing, one, two, three, four" into a microphone to determine whether his equipment is working properly. The intended effects have nothing to do with the meaning of the utterance; it has no illocutionary force, and the realization of its effects has nothing to do with the hearer's recognition of the speaker's intentions. The performance of an utterance act by itself does not constitute communication. Utterance acts become communication only when they are perceived by the speaker and hearer as the realization of actions at a higher level in the communicative-action hierarchy.

Concept activation actions are generalized referring actions whereby a speaker, by a combination of physical and linguistic actions, communicates his intention to refer to an object. The linguistic devices the speaker uses to communicate his referential intentions are descriptions realized as noun phrases; the physical devices include pointing and gestures. In general, the linguistic meaning of a description does not by itself determine its reference, even in conjunction with communicative pointing and gestures, which is why intention recognition is so important to the process of planning and understanding referring expressions.

An illocutionary act consists of making an utterance with the intention that the hearer *recognize the speaker's intention* of performing the act by virtue of the relationship between the meaning of the utterance and the proposition the speaker intended the hearer to recognize. Informing and requesting are the two illocutionary acts that KAMP plans; they will be discussed in detail in this chapter.

A surface speech act is uttering a sentence with the intention of having the hearer recognize it as the realization of an illocutionary act. For example, saying *that* a particular cat is on a particular mat is an illocutionary act. It is a surface speech act to utter a sentence like "The cat is on the mat" (or, perhaps "Felix is on my welcome mat," if the concept activation actions are performed differently) with the intention of informing the hearer that the cat is on the mat. DECLARE, ASK, and COMMAND are the three types of surface speech acts planned by KAMP, corresponding to declarative, interrogative, and imperative sentences, respectively.

Stating the effects of illocutionary acts in terms of the hearer's recognition of the speaker's intentions is important, because the process of understanding an utterance frequently requires interpreting the speaker's intentions behind the action. Allen (1978) designed a language-understanding system (or perhaps more appropriately, since it did not actually interpret English sentences, a surface-speech-act interpreter) that would infer the speaker's intended illocutionary act, given a description of a speaker's surface speech act and some knowledge about the speaker's intentions. For example, if a speaker asked the attendant at an information booth, "Where is the train to Montreal?" the Allen's system would infer that the speaker probably wanted to meet the train when it came in, so it would respond by furnishing both the time and place of its arrival, since that would maximally facilitate what it believed to be the hearer's plan. Allen claims that understanding underlying intentions is the key to interpreting such indirect speech acts as, "Do you know what time it is?"

From a theoretical standpoint, it is also important for the hearer to believe that the speaker wants to convey his intentions through the hearer's understanding of the meaning of the utterance. This condition may seem obvious, but ignoring it can lead to problems. For example, consider a situation (Searle, 1969) in which I want to impress someone (who is totally ignorant of French but who can identify it by its phonetic characteristics) by making him believe I am a fluent speaker of French. I could just inform him of this fact by performing an ordinary illocutionary act — i.e. by saying "I speak French." Another way to instill this belief would be to say some utterance in French, even though he does not understand its meaning. Because the hearer does not understand the utterance, any utterance would do as well as any other to achieve the desired effect, as long as it was in French. Therefore, I could cause the hearer to believe I spoke French by uttering some irrelevant sentence like "La plume de ma tante est sur la table." One cannot classify this utterance as an illocutionary act because its intended effect has no relation to the meaning of the utterance. Since any French utterance would be adequate for the purpose, I could have just as well have said "Je parle français," which literally means, "I speak French." In this case, I have caused the hearer to believe that I speak French by producing an utterance that literally means "I speak French," but this case is really no different from the case of the irrelevant sentence. There are many possiblities for influencing someone's mental state using language. A speaker can wake someone up, frighten him, or convince him that he speaks French by saying something, but without performing an illocutionary act. In this book we are considering only those utterances that constitute true communication, and therefore entail the performance of illocutionary acts, ingoring situations similar to the above example.

The theory adopted here assumes that the following relationship holds among illocutionary acts, perlocutionary effects, and utterances: the speaker intends to achieve a goal that he reasons can be brought about by the perlocutionary effects of a particular illocutionary act performed in the current context. The speaker then plans a surface speech act with the right force and propositional content. The hearer recognizes the surface speech act by knowing the propositional content and illocutionary force of the utterance, and infers what illocutionary act the speaker intended to perform. From the hearer's knowledge of the conventions governing illocutionary acts, the mutual knowledge he shared with the speaker, and his knowledge of the speaker's intentions, he changes his beliefs or intentions. Ideally these changes will correspond to the perlocutionary effects for which the speaker originally planned the action.

5.2 The role of illocutionary acts in speech act theory

The theory on which KAMP is built depends to a major extent on the role of illocutionary acts in the intention recognition process. The effects of the illocutionary act are realized by the hearer's recognition that the act is intentional. The hearer directly recognizes a speaker's DECLARE, ASK, and COMMAND actions, and from these surface speech acts reasons about which illocutionary act was intended. The one actually recognized is the choice that determines what perlocutionary effects will result.

Cohen and Levesque (1980) suggest that the level of description of speech acts characterized by illocutionary acts is really redundant. If the right assumptions are made about the mutual knowledge and shared plans of the agents, one can reason directly from the effects of a surface speech act to the intended perlocutionary effects without having to recognize any intermediate illocutionary acts. Cohen and Levesque show how one can define illocutionary acts such as REQUEST and COMMAND as macro-operators that expand into a sequence of lower-level actions and inferences based on mutual belief. However, these macroactions do not have to be recognized explicitly as such to exert their intended effects on the hearer.

This theory makes illocutionary acts unnecessary for a theory of speech acts. It also eliminates the distinction between direct and indirect speech acts, because this differentiation depends on the relationship between the intended illocutionary act and the surface speech act that is part of the latter's execution. Since illocutionary acts play no role, the only distinction between a direct and indirect speech act is the length of the chain of inferences leading from the surface speech act to the recognition of the speaker's intention.

Despite the elegance of this theory, illocutionary acts are still useful for planning for a number of reasons. Most importantly, they provide a convenient level of abstraction at which a planner can reason about recognition of communicative intentions without actually having to construct the details of a surface utterance. It has been demonstrated by STRIPS (Fikes and Nilsson, 1971) that macro operators can be useful in formulating complex plans, and illocutionary acts are a type of macro operator. Cohen and Levesque point out that illocutionary act descriptions may play a role in formalizing the semantics of illocutionary verbs. But, Cohen and Levesque's theory does not take into account the manner in which indirect speech acts achieve such goals as politeness. What seems to be relevant to such social goals is *how* a particular illocutionary act is performed at the surface level, given the choices available (Lakoff, 1973). It is important, therefore, for the hearer to know *which* illocutionary act is being performed, and to decide if it is being performed in an appropriate way. Since there remains considerable justification on both theoretical and practical grounds for maintaining the level of illocutionary acts in the abstraction hierarchy of linguistic actions, such actions continue to play a salient role in KAMP's planning process.

5.3   Formalizing Illocutionary Acts

One of the central problems of utterance planning is devising a formalism for illocutionary acts that not only captures the essence of what it means to perform an illocutionary act, but is also sufficiently straightforward to enable a planner to reason with it efficiently.

The first attempt at such a formalization was made by Cohen (1978). Cohen's formalization of illocutionary acts is a reasonably straightforward rendition in logic of Searle's conditions for the successful performance of various illocutionary acts (Searle, 1969). Cohen divided his preconditions into two groups: *want preconditions,* i.e., conditions on the speaker's intentions, and *can do* preconditions, which covered all other prerequisites. The effects of illocutionary acts were formalized as the hearer's awareness that the speaker wants him to believe something or do something. To bridge the gap between the illocutionary effect and the intended perlocutionary effect, Cohen proposed formal "actions" that would accomplish this purpose. For example, if the goal was **Believe**(H, P), Cohen's planner would plan an illocutionary act $\text{Do}(S, \text{Inform}(H, P))$ that would produce as an effect

(5.1) $\text{Believe}(H, \textbf{Want}(S, \textbf{Believe}(H, P)))$

Since it is impossible for a speaker to influence a hearer's beliefs directly, Cohen proposed a formal action called CONVINCE that represented the process whereby the hearer accepts as true the proposition of the speaker's utterance. CONVINCE has the formula in 5.1 as a precondition and produces the desired hearer belief as the effect. The CONVINCE action was really a short cut around axiomatizing the process of how an agent is willing to believe something given that he knows someone else intends him to believe it. In the KAMP formalism, the effects of actions are stated in terms of knowledge about knowledge and therefore CONVINCE is unnecessary. If the formalism were recast in terms of belief, then axioms would be required to specify when an agent is willing to believe something he knows that another agent believes. This approach is better than having an action like CONVINCE because CONVINCE is a summary of a chain of reasoning rather than an action performed by the speaker.

In axiomatizing illocutionary acts, as is the case with axiomatizing any facts about the world, it is necessary to choose some level of description detail that both captures the essential properties of the concepts one wishes to reason about, while simultaneously avoiding detail that is incommensurate with the level of abstraction at which the actions are being described. In the case of illocutionary acts, this decision amounts to assigning the role of recognition of intention in the speech-act-understanding process. It simplifies the planning process to eliminate recognition of intention entirely, but to do so limits the system's adaptability for dealing with certain kinds of situations, such as indirect speech acts. On the other hand, although greatly complicating the reasoning process, reliance on recognition of intention gives the system considerable flexibility and more closely models the performance of humans. Of course, for an adquate theoretical account of speech acts, one must demonstrate that the most difficult cases are handled correctly.

Let us consider some attempts to axiomatize the effects of the INFORM action. This is performed by the speaker S, who intends to achieve the perlocutionary effect that a hearer H will know that a proposition P is true. The simplest initial attempt at an axiomatization is to state that the result of an informing action such as $\mathrm{Do}(S, \mathrm{Inform}(H, P))$ is simply **Believe**(H, P). This axiomatization involves no recognition of intention, and so cannot be the description of a communicative act. Perhaps this axiom would describe adequately what would happen if S could hook some electrodes to H's brain and, by sending the right electronic signals, could cause H to believe P.

The most obvious shortcoming of this simple analysis is that (among other things) it is impossible to conclude that a hearer will not believe something he is told. In some task oriented situations, however, the simple analysis is not so far from the truth that it is useless. Consider, for example, a task-oriented dialogue in which an expert with extensive domain knowledge is assisting an apprentice who knows relatively little. The apprentice usually believes what the expert says if he has no reason to suspect he is being misled. By the same token, the expert always believes the sincerity of the apprentice's requests and always endeavors to cooperate. Therefore, when operating in such situations, adopting an action summary for INFORM that suggests a direct link between informing and believing may be useful for simplifying the planner's search.

A modification of the simple analysis, with a view to modeling the speaker's ability to reason about whether an assertion will be believed by the hearer, defines the effects of informing as

$$\mathbf{Know}(H, \mathbf{Believe}(H, P)).$$

This means that the hearer knows that the speaker believes P. This allows one to state axioms describing the kind of situation in which one agent believes something he knows another agent believes, such as "A judge will believe the testimony of a witness if the judge knows that the witness was at the scene of the crime."

A further refinement is to include recognition of intention in the definition of the illocutionary act. The effect of $\mathrm{Do}(S, \mathrm{Inform}(H, P))$ is

$$\mathbf{Know}(H, \mathbf{Intend}(S, \mathbf{Believe}(H, P))).$$

This definition expedites the incorporation of plan recognition into the model because intention is explicitly mentioned. It is then possible to axiomatize the process whereby the hearer draws conclusions about why the speaker wants him to believe P, as well as about the truth of P itself.

One of the desirable features of the KAMP system is that these different levels of axiomatization of illocutionary acts can be combined to the overall advantage of the system. Action summaries are based on the simpler effects; the more complex effects involving intention recognition are described by the axioms the deduction system employs to reason about the way the world has changed as a result of an action. Since a large number of common cases will be covered by the basic actions encoded in the action summaries, the process of verification will often succeed without encountering any problems. In the relatively small number of cases in which the action summaries are inadequate, clues are provided by the failure of the proof as to what went wrong and how the deficiency could be corrected. Thus, KAMP gains the heuristic advantages of the simpler axiomatizations without sacrificing any of the generality of the more complex axiomatizations.

As is the case with the other actions described in Chapter 3, the preconditions and effects of illocutionary acts are assumed to be universal knowledge. The formalization of INFORM is similar to that proposed for physical actions in Chapter 3. Several axioms are needed: one to state the preconditions of informing, one to state the physical effects of the action, one to state the effect of the action on the mutual knowledge of the speaker and hearer, and, finally, a "knowledge state frame axiom" to describe the effect on the knowledge of other agents that may be unaware that the action has taken place. As is the case when one is describing the knowledge effects of physical actions, the knowledge effects of illocutionary acts can be deduced from general world knowledge combined with the implicitly represented fact that all agents know what it means to inform.

In the following axioms, A and B are the speaker and hearer, respectively, w_1 is the world in which the action is performed, w_2 is the world resulting from the action, and P is a variable ranging over object language terms that denote truth-values. Axiom 5.2 describes the preconditions of informing:

$$
\begin{aligned}
(5.2) \quad \forall A, B, P, w_1, w_2 \; R(&\text{:Do}(A, \text{:Inform}(B, P)), w_1, w_2) \supset \\
& V(w_1, \text{:Location}(A)) = V(w_1, \text{:Location}(B)) \wedge \\
& T(w_1, \mathbf{Intend}(@(A), \mathbf{Know}(@(B), @(P)))) \wedge \\
& T(w_1, \mathbf{Know}(@(A), @(P))).
\end{aligned}
$$

Axiom 5.2 says that, if A informs B that P, then A and B must be at the same location (a physical enabling condition), A must intend B to know P, and A must know himself that P is true (sincerity condition).

It is assumed here that informing (and the performance of illocutionary acts

in general) does not alter the physical state of the world. Therefore, informing has
no physical effects, and frame axioms state that everything that was true before
the action will also be true after the action, and that the values of all terms remain
the same. This is expressed by axiom 5.3:

$$(5.3) \quad \forall A, B, P, w_1, w_2, \; R(:\mathrm{Do}(A, :\mathrm{Inform}(B, P)), w_1, w_2) \supset$$
$$\forall q \, H(w_1, q) \equiv H(w_2, q) \land \forall x \, V(w_1, x) = V(w_2, x).$$

Surprisingly, the axiom that describes the knowledge effects of INFORM is
very simple, since all it needs to state is that the speaker and hearer are mutually
aware of the action. Axiom 5.4 is essentially the same as the axioms describing the
knowledge effects of such actions as reading and moving, as discussed in Chapter 4.

$$(5.4) \quad \forall A, B, P, w_1, w_2 \; R(:\mathrm{Do}(A, :\mathrm{Inform}(B, P)), w_1, w_2) \supset$$
$$\forall w_3 \, K(\mathrm{Kernel}(A, B), w_2, w_3) \supset$$
$$\exists w_4 \, K(\mathrm{Kernel}(A, B), w_1, w_4) \land$$
$$R(:\mathrm{Do}(A, :\mathrm{Inform}(B, P)), w_4, w_3).$$

Given precondition Axiom 5.2, it is possible to deduce that, after A has performed
the informing action, A and B mutually know that prior to the action (1) A
intended B to know P and (2) A himself knew that P. Given this information,
it is possible to deduce that, after the action has taken place, B knows P. In
this simplified axiom, the perlocutionary effect of B's knowing P follows from
Axiom 3.2, which asserts that what is known is true. If **Know** were replaced by
Believe, other, probably more complex axioms would be required for deducing
the perlocutionary effects.

In addition to the above axioms, 5.2, 5.3, and 5.4, an action summary for
KAMP must be written. This summary will reflect the physical preconditions of
the action, as well as the basic knowledge-state preconditions, and also state as the
effect of the action that B knows P, thus allowing the planner, in its first attempt
to formulate a plan, to bypass the potentially complex process of reasoning about
perlocutionary effects. Each action axiomatized for KAMP requires an action
summary. The one for INFORM was discussed in Chapter 4.

The axiomatization of REQUEST is quite similar to the axiomatization of INFORM, and, as was the case with the latter, a choice can be made among several levels of detail of intention recognition. Although it is reasonable to define a REQUEST action in which the hearer is requested to make a proposition true, the only case considered here is one in which a REQUEST involves some future action by the hearer. Therefore, the arguments to REQUEST are the intended hearer and an intensional description of the action. The simplest description of REQUEST states that the effect of A_1's asking A_2 to do E is that A_2 intends to do E. This suffers from the same problem that confronted the oversimplified definition of INFORM, namely, that it precludes any refusal of the request by A_2. A more realistic axiomatization would have as its effect

$$\mathbf{Know}(A_2, \mathbf{Intend}(A_1, \mathbf{Intend\text{-}To\text{-}Do}(A_2, E))).$$

In this case one also needs some sort of "helpfulness axiom" that would allow one to conclude $\mathbf{Intend\text{-}To\text{-}Do}(A_2, E)$ from

$$\mathbf{Know}(A_2, \mathbf{Intend}(A_1, \mathbf{Intend\text{-}To\text{-}Do}(A_2, E))).$$

Given the above analysis, REQUEST is axiomatized in a manner similar to other actions in the possible-worlds formalism.

Preconditions:

(5.5) $\forall A, B, E, w_1, w_2\, R(:\mathrm{Do}(A, :\mathrm{Request}(B, E)), w_1, w_2) \supset$

$$V(w_1, :\mathrm{Location}(A)) = V(w_1, :\mathrm{Location}(B)) \wedge$$

$$T(w_1, \mathbf{Intend}(@(A), \mathbf{Intend\text{-}To\text{-}Do}(@(B), @(E)))).$$

Physical effects:

(5.6) $\qquad \forall A, B, E, w_1, w_2\, R(:\mathrm{Do}(A, :\mathrm{Request}(B, E)), w_1, w_2) \supset$

$$\forall z\, V(w_2, z) = V(w_1, z) \wedge$$

$$\forall p\, H(w_2, p) \equiv H(w_1, p).$$

Knowledge effects:

(5.7) $\qquad \forall A, B, E, w_1, w_2\, R(:\mathrm{Do}(A, :\mathrm{Request}(B, E)), w_1, w_2) \supset$

94

$$\forall w_3 \, K(\text{Kernel}(A, B), w_2, w_3) \supset$$
$$\exists w_4 \, [K(\text{Kernel}(A, B), w_1, w_4) \wedge$$
$$R(:\text{Do}(A, :\text{Request}(B, E)), w_4, w_3)].$$

Helpfulness axiom:

(5.8) $\forall A, B, P, w \, T(w, \text{Helpfully-Disposed}(@(A), @(B))) \equiv$
$$T(w, \text{Know}(@(A), \text{Intend}(@(B), \text{Intend-To-Do}(@(A), @(E))))) \supset$$
$$T(w, \text{Intend-To-Do}(@(A), @(E))).$$

The axioms 5.5–5.8 provide the necessary knowledge for drawing conclusions about agent B's intentions after A makes a request.[6]

5.4 Planning questions

The description of the INFORM action in Axioms 5.2–5.4 describes what happens when one agent informs another *that* a proposition is true. There are two similar additional actions that must be considered: (1) an agent informs another about the referent of a description, and (2) an agent informs another *whether* a proposition is true. The first action is what an agent wants when he asks a wh-question, while the second is what he is requesting with a yes-no question.

The problem is that, when an agent plans to ask a question, part of the specification of the action he is requesting is unknown. Therefore, the action summaries, which were designed with the expectation of fully instantiated goals, do not properly match the goal the planner is trying to satisfy. When a wh-question is planned, the goal that motivates the request is

$$T(w, \exists x \, \text{Know}(A, D = x)).$$

The action summary for INFORM matches

$$T(w, \text{Know}(A, P))$$

but does not match the wff with the broadly scoped existential quantifier. A

95

similar problem arises with yes-no questions when the agent must plan an action that results in

$$\mathbf{Know}(A, P) \vee \mathbf{Know}(A, \neg P).$$

The action summary for INFORM matches either one of the two disjuncts, but not the entire formula. The planner, in attempting to achieve such a goal, would plan a disjunctive split with one branch for each disjunct. On one branch, one agent would request that the other agent inform him that P and, on the other branch, that he inform him that $\neg P$. This is not what was intended, because a yes-no question does not request a particular answer unless some strong presuppositions have been communicated.

The solution (originally proposed by Allen (1978) and Cohen (1978)) is to have two additional informing actions that do not mention in their syntax any of the missing information that must be furnished. Consequently, an INFORMREF action is defined that does not directly mention the coreferring description being requested, and an INFORMIF action is defined that produces as its effect the disjunction

$$\mathbf{Know}(A, P) \vee \mathbf{Know}(A, \neg P).$$

KAMP treats INFORMREF and INFORMIF as essentially primitive actions for agents who are not doing the planning, since the planning agent need not concern himself with the details of their realization. He need only be able to reason about their ultimate effects on his knowledge.

Axioms 5.9–5.11 describe the INFORMREF action in the possible worlds formalism:

Preconditions:

(5.9) $\forall A, B, D, w_1, w_2 \, R(:\!\mathrm{Do}(A, :\!\mathrm{Informref}(B, D)), w_1, w_2) \supset$
$$V(w_1, :\!\mathrm{Location}(A)) = V(w1, :\!\mathrm{Location}(B)) \wedge$$
$$T(w_1, \mathbf{Intend}(@(A), \mathbf{Knowref}(@(B), @(D)))) \wedge$$
$$T(w_1, \mathbf{Knowref}(@(A), @(D))).$$

Physical effects:

(5.10) $\forall A, B, D, w_1, w_2, \, R(:\!\mathrm{Do}(A, :\!\mathrm{Informref}(B, D)), w_1, w_2) \supset$

$$\forall q\, H(w_1, q) \equiv H(w_2, q) \wedge \forall x\, V(w_1, x) = V(w_2, x).$$

Knowledge effects:

(5.11) $\forall A, B, D, w_1, w_2\, R(:\mathrm{Do}(A, :\mathrm{Informref}(B, D)), w_1, w_2) \supset$

     $\forall w_3\, K(\mathrm{Kernel}(A, B), w_2, w_3) \supset [\exists w_4\, K(\mathrm{Kernel}(A, B), w_1, w_4) \wedge$

     $R(:\mathrm{Do}(A, :\mathrm{Informref}(B, D)), w_4, w_3)].$

     Axioms 5.12–5.14 describe the INFORMIF action.

Preconditions:

(5.12) $\forall A, B, P, w_1, w_2\, R(:\mathrm{Do}(A, :\mathrm{Informif}(B, P)), w_1, w_2) \supset$

     $V(w_1, :\mathrm{Location}(A)) = V(w_1, :\mathrm{Location}(B)) \wedge$

     $T(w_1, \mathbf{Intend}(@(A), \mathbf{Know}(@(B), @(P)) \vee \mathbf{Know}(@(B), \neg@(P)))) \wedge$

     $T(w_1, \mathbf{Know}(@(B), @(P)) \vee \mathbf{Know}(@(B), \neg@(P))).$

Physical effects:

(5.13) $\forall A, B, P, w_1, w2,\, R(:\mathrm{Do}(A, :\mathrm{Informif}(B, P)), w_1, w_2) \supset$

     $\forall q\, H(w_1, q) \equiv H(w_2, q) \wedge \forall x\, V(w_1, x) = V(w_2, x).$

Knowledge effects:

(5.14) $\forall A, B, P, w_1, w_2\, R(:\mathrm{Do}(A, :\mathrm{Informif}(B, P)), w_1, w_2) \supset$

     $\forall w_3\, K(\mathrm{Kernel}(A, B), w_2, w3) \supset [\exists w_4\, K(\mathrm{Kernel}(A, B), w_1, w_4) \wedge$

     $R(:\mathrm{Do}(A, :\mathrm{Informif}(B, P)), w_4, w_3)].$

5.5   Conclusion

This chapter has shown how illocutionary acts can be axiomatized within Moore's possible-worlds-semantics formalism for reasoning about knowledge and action, and how the resulting axiomatization can be used efficiently by KAMP to generate plans. The essential idea was to axiomatize illocutionary acts as actions resulting in the knowledge that they have been performed. This, together with conditions on the speaker's knowledge and intentions that are expressed by the axioms as preconditions, enable the hearer to reason about what the speaker intends and knows.

Action summaries provide a simpler level of description of the same action; this description facilitates the heuristic generation of plans involving illocutionary acts. The next chapter on planning of surface linguistic actions examines the question of how illocutionary acts are realized as actual utterances.

6
Planning surface linguistic acts

6.1 Introduction

This chapter discusses the problems of planning surface linguistic actions, including *surface speech acts, concept activation actions,* and *focusing actions.* What distinguishes these surface linguistic acts from the illocutionary acts considered in Chapter 5 is that they correspond directly to parts of the utterance that are produced by the planning agent. An agent intends to convey a proposition by performing an illocutionary act. There may be many choices available to him for the purpose of conveying the proposition with the intended illocutionary force. For example, he may make a direct request by using an imperative, or perform the act of requesting indirectly by asking a question. He usually has many options available to him for referring to objects in the world.

A surface linguistic act, on the other hand, represents *a particular linguistic realization* of the intended illocutionary act. Planning a surface speech act entails making choices about the many options that are left open by a high-level specification of an illocutionary act. In addition, the surface speech act must satisfy a multitude of constraints imposed by the grammar of the language. The domain of reasoning done by the planner includes actions along with their preconditions and effects. The grammatical constraints lie outside this domain of actions and goals (excluding, of course, the implicit goal of producing coherent English), and are therefore most suitably specified within a different system. However, it is impossible to completely separate these two domains of reasoning. For example, a planner devising a plan to refer to an object may choose a certain set of descriptors. It may be the case that these descriptors can be realized only by a set of clauses, perhaps resulting in a sentence with a heavy, awkward noun phrase that is difficult to understand. On the other hand, the planner could attempt to devise an alternative set of descriptors that would also communicate the right referring intention, but do so by means of a simpler, more felicitous sentence. To produce a sentence it is necessary to reason simultaneously both regarding what is known about the world and what is linguistically possible.

This chapter addresses the problems of coordinating the linguistic and planning knowledge required to make decisions like the one just described. The issues to be explored include the integration of grammatical knowledge with the planner, the axiomatization of surface speech acts, concept activation actions, focusing, centering, and the performance of multiple illocutionary acts by means of a single surface speech act.

6.2 Surface speech acts

Surface speech acts were introduced in Chapter 5 to serve as an abstract representation of utterances. There is a one-to-one correspondence between surface speech acts and utterances, since the former are merely abstract representations of the latter. No such simple correspondence holds between illocutionary acts and utterances.

Direct realization as a surface speech act is only *one* possible strategy for the expansion of an illocutionary act. It is the most important one, however because almost all illocutionary acts are either realized directly as surface speech acts or incorporated into other surface speech acts through action subsumption (discussed in Section 6.9).

Corresponding to the three fundamental sentential mood choices in English, there are three types of surface speech acts: COMMAND, realized by imperative sentences, ASK, realized by interrogative sentences and ASSERT, realized by declarative sentences. The effect of a surface speech act is that the speaker and the hearer mutually know that the action has taken place. This knowledge leads the hearer to infer that the speaker intended him to recognize that a particular illocutionary act has been performed, which in turn leads the hearer to alter his beliefs and intentions, thus bringing about the perlocutionary effects for which the action was planned.

The connection between surface speech acts and the illocutionary acts that underlie them is complex for two reasons: (1) the same surface speech act can be recognized as the realization of any one of a number of illocutionary acts, depending on the context in which it is uttered; (2) it is possible for a single surface speech act to realize several illocutionary acts. A surface speech act could realize one action in one context and several actions in another, given a different set of speaker and hearer beliefs. To describe the relationship between surface speech acts and illocutionary acts in its full potentiality would require a description of the reasoning processes by means of which the hearer establishes this connection. As a first step in this direction, the simplest case of axiomatizing direct speech acts is considered in Section 6.6, while some of the possibilities for expanding this treatment to more general cases are examined in Section 6.10. However, much work remains to be done in this area. Cohen and Levesque (1980) have considered many of the problems entailed in axiomatizing surface speech acts and the knowledge used to interpret them.

6.3   The role of grammatical knowledge

Levy (1979b) cites three ways of viewing a text: in terms of its content, as an activity, and as an object. The plan-based theory embodied in KAMP accounts for the content of utterances and their role as intentional communicative activity. The plan-based account is less successful, however, in describing the utterance as an object — i.e., in specifying the intricacies of syntactic structure and the constraints that apply to well-formed sentences. From this perspective it is more natural to view a sentence as a complex artifact designed to satisfy a set of specifications, rather than as an utterance act.

Nevertheless, it is also important to consider the utterance from the perspective of action because many of the artifact design choices are made with the intention of getting the hearer to recognize the speaker's intention to perform a particular action. For example, one syntactic structure may be preferred to another because the selected structure is considered more appropriate for communicating a desired shift in focus.

Because of this action-artifact duality, the grammar must be designed in a manner that makes it possible to represent linguistic knowledge perspicuously, while at the same time providing the information needed by the planner to relate syntactic choices to the action that is intended to be recognized.

KAMP was originally implemented with a grammar of simple context-free rules. These rules were used to generate a syntactic-structure tree that was associated with the node in the procedural network representing the associated surface speech act. NP nodes in the tree were associated with concept activation actions in the network. Critics that proposed modification of the plan would be required to check to verify that the changes in the syntactic structure implied by the changes in the plan still resulted in a grammatical sentence.

This approach was judged inadequate because of it lacked modularity and perspicuity. Some grammatical knowledge was represented as conditions and actions within the planning modules that bear responsibility for making particular grammatical decisions. Other grammatical knowledge was embedded in the critics and in the rules that generated the basic syntax tree. The only motivation for this distribution of knowledge was convenience of implementation. It became clear that, if the linguistic capabilities of KAMP were to be extended beyond the most trivial, a more coherent grammatical representation and a cleaner interface between the grammar and the planner had to be developed.

Subsequent research led to the development of TELEGRAM (an acronym for **Tele**ological **Gram**mar) (Appelt, 1983), which provides for a separation between the processes that view the utterance as action and those that view it as an artifact, while still permitting adequate communication between them. The TELEGRAM acronym arises from the fact that it is a grammar designed to facilitate goal satisfaction.

It would be appropriate, at this juncture, to reiterate the research goals of KAMP. The KAMP system was designed to furnish a framework for planning utterances, to test the feasibility of that framework to model the process whereby speakers plan utterances that satisfy multiple goals. It was not an objective of this research to write a grammar with broad, robust linguistic coverage. Consequently, the TELEGRAM grammar has not yet been developed to the point at which it deserves recognition for its complete and robust coverage of the English language. It was rather designed to test its viability as a fundamental grammar formalism with which more extensive efforts to combine linguistic reasoning and planning can be undertaken in the future.

6.4   Unification grammar and functional descriptions

TELEGRAM is based on the ideas of *functional unification grammar* (known also as unification grammar or UG) described by Kay (1979, 1981). Unification grammar is one of a set of related linguistic formalisms including lexical-functional grammar (Kaplan and Bresnan, 1980), the PATR-II formalism (Shieber, 1984), generalized phrase structure grammar (Gazdar and Pullum, 1982) and definite-clause grammar (Pereira and Warren, 1980). Although these grammar formalisms differ in their details, they share many common underlying ideas. One of the most important underlying notions is that syntactic categories are best characterized by collections of features. Certain syntactic relationships, including dominance and precedence, can hold between two constituents only if certain of their sets of features are compatible. This compatibility is determined by an operation called *unification,* described in detail below. In the case of definite-clause grammars, rules are expressed as Horn clauses; unification in this case is the familiar unification operation used by all resolution theorem provers (Manna, 1974). The other grammars use attribute-value pairs for indexing features rather than position in a clause, but aside from this minor difference, however, the operation is essentially the same as unification in logic.

Kay's formalism has special appeal for generation systems because of the way syntactic structures are specified. Hierarchical tree structure is best suited for parsing and interpretation. UG employs a much flatter structure of ordering constraints and, while not as suitable for parsing as other grammatical formalisms, it is particularly well suited to generation because of the emphasis on the functional roles of constituents. In addition to TELEGRAM, UG has been successfully employed by McKeown's generation system (1982) for answering questions about database structure.

All linguistic entities in UG are characterized by collections of features. The objects described by such a collection are those that share just those particular features. The empty description applies to all objects, while the unification of two descriptions applies to the intersection of the objects to which each description applies. A *functional description* (FD) consists of a possibly empty set of *patterns* together with a collection of features and their associated values. Patterns are regular expressions that describe how the values of certain features in the FD are combined to form a syntactic structure. Figure 6.1 illustrates an FD that describes the sentence "He saw her." An FD may include a disjunction of a set of features, in which case the FD denotes those expressions that contain *any one* of them.

In this notation, square brackets indicate a conjunction of the enclosed features. Two sets of features so designated will unify only if each of their corresponding components unifies. Braces denote disjunction of features. Angle brackets provide a way of referring to other features in a FD. < X > denotes the value of the X feature in the current functional description. < X Y > denotes the value of the Y feature of the X feature in the current description. <↑ X > denotes the value of the X feature of the FD of which the current FD is a part. The "=" operator means "unifies with," and similarly, "≠" means "does not unifiy with."

For example, in Figure 6.1 the REFERENT feature of the subject noun phrase specifies <↑ AGENT > as its value. The value of the AGENT feature from the immediately superior FD is < PROPCONT ARG1 >. In turn, this value specifies PERSON1. Note that the value of the PROPCONT feature is merely the propositional content expressed in attribute-value notation rather than the more familiar predicate-argument notation.

The PAT feature is special because its value is assumed to be a pattern that tells how to combine features of the functional description to form an actual utterance. A pattern is really a regular expression over an alphabet consisting of the features associated with the constituent in which the pattern appears. For example the pattern

$$(\ldots < \text{SUBJ} > \ldots < \text{VERB} > \ldots < \text{OBJ} > \ldots)$$

indicates that the surface structure it describes is constrained by the fact that the constituent described by the SUBJ feature must precede (optionally with some intervening constituents) the constituent described by the VERB feature.[7]

$$
\begin{bmatrix}
\text{CAT} = \text{S} \\
\text{PAT} = (\ldots < \text{SUBJ} >< \text{AUX} >< \text{VERB} >< \text{OBJ} > \ldots) \\
\text{AGENT} = < \text{PROPCONT ARG1} > \\
\text{GOAL} = < \text{PROPCONT ARG2} > \\
\text{SUBJ} = \begin{bmatrix}
\text{CAT} = \text{NP} \\
\text{PAT} = (\ldots < \text{HEAD} > \ldots) \\
\text{REFERENT} = <\uparrow \text{AGENT} > \\
\text{AGR} = < \text{HEAD AGR} > \\
\text{HEAD} = \begin{bmatrix}
\text{CAT} = \text{PRO} \\
\text{PNAME} = \text{``he''} \\
\text{AGR} = \begin{bmatrix} \text{PER} = \text{3RD} \\ \text{NBR} = \text{SING} \end{bmatrix} \\
\text{GENDER} = \text{MASC} \\
\text{CASE} = \text{NOM}
\end{bmatrix}
\end{bmatrix} \\
\text{OBJ} = \begin{bmatrix}
\text{CAT} = \text{NP} \\
\text{AGR} = < \text{HEAD AGR} > \\
\text{REFERENT} = <\uparrow \text{GOAL} > \\
\text{PAT} = (\ldots < \text{HEAD} > \ldots) \\
\text{HEAD} = \begin{bmatrix}
\text{CAT} = \text{PRO} \\
\text{PNAME} = \text{``her''} \\
\text{AGR} = \begin{bmatrix} \text{PER} = \text{3RD} \\ \text{NBR} = \text{SING} \end{bmatrix} \\
\text{GENDER} = \text{FEM} \\
\text{CASE} = \text{ACC}
\end{bmatrix}
\end{bmatrix} \\
\text{VERB} = \begin{bmatrix}
\text{CAT} = \text{V} \\
\text{PNAME} = \text{``see''} \\
\text{AGR} = <\uparrow \text{SUBJ AGR} > \\
\text{PRED} = \text{SEE}
\end{bmatrix} \\
\text{PROPCONT} = \begin{bmatrix}
\text{PRED} = \text{SEE} \\
\text{ARG1} = \text{PERSON1} \\
\text{ARG2} = \text{PERSON2}
\end{bmatrix} \\
\text{TENSE} = \text{PAST} \\
\text{VOICE} = \text{ACTIVE} \\
\text{AUX} = \text{NIL}
\end{bmatrix}
$$

Figure 6.1: Functional Description for *He saw her*

Note that in the functional description in Figure 6.1 the value of the AUX feature is NIL. This means that the functional description does not specify any value for it. Therefore, the FD in Figure 6.1 also describes the sentences *He was seeing her, He had been seeing her,* and *He had seen her.* If one desired to restrict the FD to specify only the sentence *He saw her,* then one would specify NONE as the value of the AUX feature, indicating that no auxiliary is present in the sentence.

The unification, F_3, of two functional descriptions F_1 and F_2, written $F_3 = F_1 \oplus F_2$ is defined as follows:

1. If $F_1 = \bigvee_{k=1}^{n} D_k$, then there is at least one functional description D_i such that $F_3 = D_i \oplus F_2$.

2. If $\langle f_1, v_1 \rangle$ is a attribute-value pair and either $\langle f_1, v_1 \rangle \in F_1$ and $\forall x (\langle f_1, x \rangle \notin F_2)$, or $\langle f_1, v_1 \rangle \in F_2$ and $\forall x (\langle f_1, x \rangle \notin F_1)$, then $\langle f_1, v_1 \rangle \in F_3$.

3. If $\langle f_1, v_1 \rangle \in F_1$ and $\langle f_1, v_2 \rangle \in F_2$, then $\langle f_1, v_3 \rangle \in F_3$ if any of the following conditions apply:

   (a) If $f_1 = \text{PAT}$, then v_3 is the intersection of the patterns specified by v_1 and v_2.

   (b) If $v_1 = v_2$, then $v_3 = v_1$

   (c) If $v_1 = \text{NIL}$, then $v_3 = v_2$ and similarly for v_2.

   (d) If $v_1 = \text{ANY}$ and $v_2 \neq \text{NONE}$, then $v_3 = v_2$ and similarly for v_2.

   (e) If v_1 and v_2 are patterns, then v_3 is a pattern denoting the intersection of the sets denoted by v_1 and v_2.

   (f) If v_1 and v_2 are functional descriptions, then $v_3 = v_1 \oplus v_2$.

4. Otherwise, the unification fails and the value of $F_1 \oplus F_2$ is undefined.

A *unification grammar* G consists of a very large functional description that specifies all the sentences of the language. A unification grammar is used for generation by constructing a functional description D of an intended sentence and then computing $G \oplus D$. The description D is supposedly a minimal collection of features specifying one or more utterances that are consistent with the speaker's intentions. The result of computing $G \oplus D$ is a complete specification and instantiation of all features associated with the utterance, so that it becomes possible to extract a sequence of lexical elements by looking at the PAT feature in $G \oplus D$.

Figure 6.2 shows the top level of a unification grammar of English. The top level consists of a disjunction of the different types of constituents. When an FD is unified with the grammar, each major constituent (any FD with a CAT feature) is also unified with the top-level grammar. This allows the grammar designer to modularize the knowledge associated with each major constituent.

Figure 6.3 shows an exerpt from TELEGRAM's grammar for noun phrases. This excerpt is included to give the reader a feeling for the way linguistic information is represented in a unification grammar. The PAT feature stipulates that a noun phrase consists of the features DET, PREMODS, HEAD, and POSTMODS, and that they are constrained to appear *in that order* if they appear at all. The NP grammar contains information that is used to determine whether or not each of these constituents can be a part of the utterance. Their detailed structure is specified elsewhere in the grammar. This grammar states that every noun phrase has a feature HEAD, which can be of category N (noun), PRO (pronoun), or SCOMP (sentential complement). If the HEAD is a proper noun, then there can be no determiner. If the head is SCOMP or PRO, the HEAD can be the only constituent of the noun phrase (ignoring such sentences as "He who hesitates is lost."). PREMODS can consist of an ADJP, which is specified elsewhere in the grammar to consist of a

$$\left[\left\{\begin{matrix} \begin{bmatrix} \text{CAT} = \text{S} \\ \vdots \end{bmatrix} \\ \begin{bmatrix} \text{CAT} = \text{NP} \\ \vdots \end{bmatrix} \\ \begin{bmatrix} \text{CAT} = \text{DET} \\ \vdots \end{bmatrix} \\ \vdots \end{matrix}\right\}\right]$$

Figure 6.2: The top level of an English unification grammar

sequence of adjectives followed by a sequence of nouns. POSTMODS can be either a relative clause or a prepositional phrase. The intricacies of quantifiers have been deferred for future development.

The NP grammar also specifies all the agreement constraints that must hold. The AGR feature of the whole NP is inherited directly from the AGR feature on the HEAD. The subject NP will in turn contribute its AGR feature to the sentence, which will be constrained to match the AGR feature of the main verb (see Figure 6.1).

6.5   The TELEGRAM grammar

Despite the advantages of UG for the representation of grammatical knowledge there are some shortcomings as well. As the formalism was originally conceived, the top-level FD must contain all the semantic information that is required to specify the intended utterance. Because the top-level FD does specify an utterance, it is natural to associate it with a surface speech-act node in the plan. However, at the time the surface speech act is first planned, the FD that can be constructed

$$
\begin{bmatrix}
\text{CAT} = \text{NP} \\
\text{PAT} = (\ldots < \text{DET} >< \text{PREMODS} >< \text{HEAD} >< \text{POSTMODS} > \ldots) \\
\text{AGR} = <\text{HEAD AGR}> \\
\left\{
\begin{array}{l}
\begin{bmatrix}
\text{HEAD} = [\text{CAT} = \text{N}] \\
\left\{
\begin{bmatrix}
\text{TYPE} = \text{PROPER} \\
\text{DET} = \text{NONE}
\end{bmatrix}
\right\} \\
\text{TYPE} = \text{COMMON}
\end{bmatrix} \\
\left\{
\begin{array}{l}
\left\{
\begin{array}{l}
\text{HEAD} = [\text{CAT} = \text{PRO}] \\
\text{HEAD} = [\text{CAT} = \text{SCOMP}]
\end{array}
\right\} \\
\text{DET} = \text{NONE} \\
\text{PREMODS} = \text{NONE} \\
\text{POSTMODS} = \text{NONE}
\end{array}
\right\}
\end{array}
\right\} \\
\left\{
\begin{array}{l}
\text{PREMODS} = \text{NONE} \\
\text{PREMODS} = [\text{CAT} = \text{ADJP}]
\end{array}
\right\} \\
\left\{
\begin{array}{l}
\text{POSTMODS} = \text{NONE} \\
\text{POSTMODS} = [\text{CAT} = \text{PP}] \\
\text{POSTMODS} = [\text{CAT} = \text{SREL}]
\end{array}
\right\}
\end{bmatrix}
$$

Figure 6.3:   A portion of the grammar for noun phrases

at that time is at best a weak constraint on the possible utterances that could be produced. For example, a surface speech act may specify an object to be referred to, but the best strategy for referring to that object has yet to be determined by the planner.

The problem with the straightforward adoption of a unification grammar as a representation of linguistic knowledge is that it encourages one to make a strong separation between the intentional and grammatical processes — the "what-how" distinction that we have been trying to avoid. As we have seen earlier in Section 1.3, the planner does not have enough information at the time the surface speech act is being planned to specify the semantics of the entire utterance. This is because linguistic information constrains the planning that leads to the fully specified FD.

Let us examine the problem of planning a description as the means of linguistic realization of a concept activation action. Choosing the right description depends primarily on reasoning about the discourse context and the mutual knowledge of the agents involved. On the basis of these considerations, the utterance planner can plan a description that can be demonstrated to communicate the right intention were it to be realized in an English sentence. All the necessary information for specifying the utterance could be included with the initial FD. However, the grammar constrains the choice of descriptors beyond what the planner would consider strictly from the standpoint of intention communication. For example, if the discourse context necessitates the use of a pronoun, the inability to include PREMODS and POSTMODS in the noun phrase means that additional descriptors cannot be planned for action subsumption. Certain predicates (e.g. color terms) can be realized as adjectives. Other more complex predicates, particularly those referring to actions and events, (e.g., "the screwdriver you used to remove the platform") can be realized only as relative clauses. If an adequate utterance is to be planned, the planner must take into account both these grammatical constraints and the requirements of intention communication. If the descriptors are selected in advance without any information about the possiblilities of linguistic realization, the planner either has to furnish a surplus of descriptors, back up and replan descriptors if constraints cannot be satisfied, or have no option left but to produce a poor utterance. Postponement of descriptor selection until more information about the entire sentence is known is clearly superior to any of these alternatives.

TELEGRAM is designed to facilitate the sharing of control and information between the planning process and the unification process. The central idea is to associate a minimal FD with the surface speech act as soon as it is inserted into the plan. This minimal FD is then unified with the grammar by means of a special unification algorithm that is capable of recognizing when it has insufficient information and invoking the planner to provide more complete information at the right time. The final result of the TELEGRAM unification is the same as if an ordinary unification algorithm had been used to unify the complete functional description with the grammar.

The TELEGRAM unifier is a function of two arguments: the first of these is always part of the utterance FD, the second always part of the grammar. The presence of a feature in the utterance FD that is not mentioned in the grammar FD is a signal to the unifier that the utterance FD is incomplete.

For example, at the time a surface speech act is initially planned, the planner knows only that a noun phrase will be required in the final utterance and that its intended referent is some object, say O_1, as depicted by the first FD in Figure 6.4. The REFERENT feature is not present in the grammar for noun phrases, and a standard unification algorithm would simply add REFERENT $= O_1$ to the unified FD. However, the TELEGRAM unifier interprets this feature as a signal that more information must be furnished by the planner. For each such feature as REFERENT, TELEGRAM associates a goal that is to be satisfied by the planner. The result of satisfying the goal will be to add more features to the FD of the intended utterance. In this case the goal will be ACTIVE(O_1) and the planner, following the strategy outlined in Section 6.7, will plan a concept activation action. The result of this planning may be a physical action, such as pointing, and a linguistic action of describing, which is reflected by the addition of the DESCRIPTION feature to the second FD in Figure 6.4.

Each predicate that is part of the description has information associated with it about how it can be realized linguistically. For example, the predicate Man(x) says

110

that in a description, it can be realized as a noun ("man") or an adjective ("male"). On the other hand, the predicate Near(x, y) can be realized only in a prepositional phrase using the prepositions "near" or "by."[8] Because the two FDs being unified are known, the planner can determine that none of the consituents of the noun phrase have been specified yet, and hence the choice of predicates is relatively unconstrained. Reasoning about mutual knowledge determines an adequate set of predicates for intention communication, and examination of the state of the functional description determines whether the predicates will be realizable in the utterance. The process described here is also used to expand the object of the prepositional phrase, finally yielding the noun phrase "the man by the window."

An additional important benefit of integrating planning and linguistic rea-

$$\begin{bmatrix} \text{CAT} = \text{NP} \\ \text{REFERENT} = O_1 \end{bmatrix}$$

$$\begin{bmatrix} \text{CAT} = \text{NP} \\ \text{REFERENT} = O_1 \\ \text{DESCRIPTION} = \lambda x \, \text{Man}(x) \wedge \text{Near}(x, \text{Window}_1) \end{bmatrix}$$

$$\begin{bmatrix} \text{CAT} = \text{NP} \\ \text{REFERENT} = O_1 \\ \text{DESCRIPTION} = \lambda x \, \text{Man}(x) \wedge \text{Near}(x, \text{Window}_1) \\ \text{DET} = \begin{bmatrix} \text{CAT} = \text{DET} \\ \text{TYPE} = \text{DEF} \\ \text{PNAME} = \text{"the"} \end{bmatrix} \\ \text{HEAD} = \begin{bmatrix} \text{CAT} = \text{N} \\ \text{PNAME} = \text{"man"} \\ \text{AGR} = [\text{NBR} = \text{SG}] \end{bmatrix} \\ \text{POSTMODS} = \begin{bmatrix} \text{CAT} = \text{PP} \\ \text{PREP} = \begin{bmatrix} \text{PNAME} = \text{"by"} \end{bmatrix} \\ \text{POBJ} = \begin{bmatrix} \text{CAT} = \text{NP} \\ \text{REFERENT} = W_1 \end{bmatrix} \end{bmatrix} \end{bmatrix}$$

Figure 6.4: Successive functional descriptions of a noun phrase

soning in the manner described is the ability to coordinate physical intention communication actions with the utterance. When the planner is reasoning about how to best communicate the speaker's intention to refer to something, it is not constrained to plan only DESCRIBE actions, but it can make any modification to the plan that it deems advisable, including the planning of physical actions. Knowledge about the communicative uses of physical actions is not the kind of knowledge that can or should be represented within a grammar, even though it plays a significant role in the design of the utterance.

The FD resulting from the augmentation produced by virtue of planning a DESCRIBE action and then continuing with the unification is the same FD that would have resulted if the entire FD had been specified and then unified with the grammar. However, by postponing some of the planning and placing it under control of the unification process, the system maintains its capacity for efficient hierarchical planning while enhancing its ability to coordinate physical and linguistic actions.

6.6 Axiomatizing surface speech acts

If surface speech acts are to be planned, the planner must have some formal description of their effects. This is not a straightforward task because a surface speech act, given the right conditions on the knowledge of the speaker and hearer, could realize a broad spectrum of illocutionary acts. Somehow the axioms must allow for the fact that "Can you pass the salt?" can be taken both as a mere question regarding the hearer's abilities and as a request to pass the salt.

Every action has prerequisites, physical effects, and knowledge-state effects. In the case of a surface speech act, the physical preconditions are enabling conditions such as being able to speak to the hearer. The knowledge preconditions depend on what illocutionary act is being performed and cannot be stated as part of the preconditions for the surface speech act. For example, if "Can you pass the salt?" is intended as a request for salt passing, it must be the case that the speaker believes the hearer can pass the salt at the time the request is made; otherwise it is not a sincere request. On the other hand, if the utterance is intended simply as a request for information, the speaker must *not* know that the hearer is indeed capable of passing the salt; otherwise the utterance is not a sincere request for information.

As is the case with other linguistic actions, surface speech acts do not have any physical effects per se. The real problems are presented in axiomatizing the knowledge effects because this is where it is necessary to specify the intention recognition conditions used by the hearer as his basis for inferring the speaker's intended illocutionary act. An initial attempt to characterize the knowledge effects of the ASSERT action is represented in Axiom 6.1.

(6.1) $$\forall A, B, w_1, w_2\ R(:\!\mathrm{Do}(A, :\!\mathrm{Assert}(B, P)), w_1, w_2) \supset$$
$$\forall w_3\ K(\mathrm{Kernel}(A, B), w_2, w_3) \supset$$
$$T(w_3, [\text{Intention recognition conditions}]) \supset$$
$$\exists w_4\ K(\mathrm{Kernel}(A, B)w_1, w_4) \wedge$$
$$R(:\!\mathrm{Do}(A, :\!\mathrm{Inform}(B, P)), w_4, w_3)$$

Axiom 6.1 states that, if A utters a declarative sentence with propositional content P, then, if A and B mutually know certain facts (called "intention-recognition conditions"), they also mutually know that A has *informed* B that P. The choice of what to specify as the intention recognition conditions determines how the relationship between declarative sentences and informing actions is characterized. If the intention recognition conditions are simply the constant "true," the axiom makes the following assertion: Whenever a speaker utters a declarative sentence with propositional content P, he informs the hearer that P. No indirect interpretations are possible. This simplified axiom was adopted in the implementation of KAMP because of the problems associated with the planning of indirect speech acts, which are described in Section 6.10.

The intention recognition conditions can be elaborated to describe the conditions on mutual knowledge under which it can be inferred that a particular illocutionary act is intended. Brown (1979) has incorporated such conditions into a system for interpreting indirect speech acts. For example, such a rule might be (in KAMP's terminology) "If the surface speech act is of the form

$$\mathrm{Do}(A, \mathrm{Ask}(B, \mathbf{Future\text{-}Occur}(\mathrm{Do}(B, Q)))),$$

113

and it is mutually believed to be consistent with A's plan to want B to do Q, then the action is a request that B do Q." An example of the application of this would be a question interpreted as a request, such as "Will you take out the garbage?" In general, such intention recognition inferences will involve reasoning both about the propositional content of the surface speech act and the mutual knowledge of the participants. The extension of KAMP along these lines is an important objective of future research.

6.7   Concept activation and referring actions

When a speaker performs any kind of surface speech act, he intends that the hearer recognize the propositional content of the utterance. This entails the hearer's constructing a proposition with terms that denote objects the speaker has in mind. The action of getting the hearer to recognize these terms is called *concept activation*. The utterance of a linguistic expression – such as a noun phrase – whose intended meaning is to denote some object in the world is *referring*. Concept activation is less constrained, since it does not necessarily rely on purely linguistic actions, but may include gestures and other physical actions with communicative intent, as well as inferentially activated concepts. An example of the latter is the utterance of "Remove the pump" in an attempt to request the hearer to remove a pump from the platform to which it is attached. Even though the platform is part of the recognized propositional content, it is not mentioned explicitly in the utterance because the speaker and hearer mutually know that the pump is attached to the platform. In this case, the concept of the platform has been activated, although the speaker has not referred to it explicitly.

KAMP divides surface speech acts into two components: *intention communication* and *linguistic realization*. The relationship between these components is illustrated in Figure 6.5. Intention communication involves planning to get the hearer to recognize that the speaker wants to do something. The linguistic realization component is concerned with realizing the actions specified by the intention communication component in a valid syntactic structure. A reciprocal channel of communication between these two components exists because the means of communication of intention determines what linguistic structures must be selected; in addition, the grammatical choices available restrict the possible means of intention communication. This channel of communication is mediated by the unification algorithm and the TELEGRAM grammar.

Currently KAMP plans only concept activation actions for which the concept is part of the speaker's and hearer's mutual knowledge. Of course, this is only one of several types of referring actions that can be realized by noun phrases. For example, one can perform an activation of a concept that is *not* shared by the speaker and hearer with the intention that the hearer identify the referent by planning to acquire sufficient information.

The goal of a concept's becoming active arises from the need to elaborate the REFERENT feature in a functional description. Axioms 6.2–6.4 describe the concept activation (:Cact) action formally.

(6.2) $\forall A, B, C, w_1, w_2 \; R(:\text{Do}(A, :\text{Cact}(\text{Kernel}(A, B), C)), w_1, w_2) \supset$

$V(w_1, :\text{Location}(A)) = V(w_1, :\text{Location}(B)) \land$

$T(w_1, \text{Intend}(@(A), \text{Mutually-Know}(@(A), @(B), \text{Active}(@(C))))))$

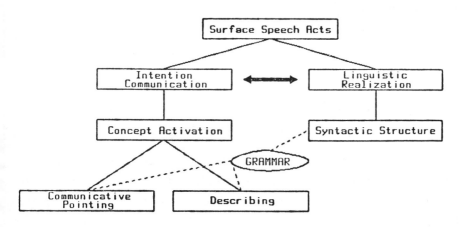

Figure 6.5:   Components of a surface speech act

(6.3) $\forall A, B, C, w_1, w_2\, R(:\mathrm{Do}(A, :\mathrm{Cact}(\mathrm{Kernel}(A,B),C)), w_1, w_2) \supset$
$\qquad H(w_2, :\mathrm{Active}(C))$

(6.4) $\forall A, B, C, w_1, w_2\, R(:\mathrm{Do}(A, :\mathrm{Cact}(\mathrm{Kernel}(A,B),C)), w_1, w_2) \supset$
$\qquad \forall w_3\, K(\mathrm{Kernel}(A,B), w_2, w_3) \supset$
$\qquad\quad \exists w_4\, K(\mathrm{Kernel}(A,B), w_1, w_4) \wedge$
$\qquad\qquad R(:\mathrm{Do}(A, :\mathrm{Cact}(\mathrm{Kernel}(A,B),C)), w_4, w_3)$

When KAMP is expanding a concept activation action to lower-level actions, it takes into account both the intention communication and linguistic realization components of the action. The intention communication component may be realized by a plan involving either physical or linguistic actions. KAMP relies on *description* as a linguistic means of communicating an intention to refer, and on *pointing* as a nonlinguistic means.

The following schema defines the preconditions of the DESCRIBE action in a manner similar to Axiom 6.2:

(6.5) $\forall A, B, w_1, w_2\, R(:\mathrm{Do}(A, :\mathrm{Describe}(B, \mathcal{D})), w_1, w_2) \supset$
$\qquad \exists x\, T(w_1, \mathbf{Know}(@(A), \mathcal{D}(@(x)))) \wedge$
$\qquad T(w_1, \neg\mathbf{Mutually\text{-}Know}(@(A), @(B), \neg\mathcal{D}^*(@(x)))) \wedge$
$\qquad T(w_1, \forall y\, \neg\mathbf{Mutually\text{-}Know}(@(A), @(B), \mathcal{D}^*(y) \supset y \neq @(x)))$

Axiom 6.5 states the preconditions for an agent A planning to use a description $\mathcal{D}$ to communicate his intention to an agent B to refer to an object. The description $\mathcal{D}$ is an object language predicate composed of a number of individual descriptors. It is defined as

$$\mathcal{D}(x) \equiv_{def} \lambda x\, (D_1(x) \wedge \ldots \wedge D_n(x)),$$

where the $D_i(x)$ are the individual descriptors that comprise the description. The

116

symbol D^* denotes a similar expression that includes all the descriptors of D conjoined with predicates that define the center of the discourse (Section 6.8). These predicates restrict the possible individuals to which the description can apply to be only those that are relevant in the current discourse context.

The first clause in the conclusion of Axiom 6.5 states that the speaker must privately know that the description that he attributes to the intended referent actually holds. The second and third clauses state that the intended referent is the only one that is not ruled out according to the mutual knowledge of the two agents. The reason for this indirect approach is that one must allow for the case in which a speaker plans a description that serves to both identify a referent and inform the hearer of properties of that referent. In that case, descriptors $D_1(x)$ through $D_i(x)$ (called the basic descriptors) will be mutually known to identify a single object, while descriptors $D_{i+1}(x)$ through $D_n(x)$ will be believed to hold of the referent only by the speaker. Therefore, when the hearer interprets the speaker's utterance with respect to their mutual knowledge, the description D is not known to apply to anything at all. However, if the speaker planned the description so that the basic descriptors are mutually known to pick out a single referent in context, then there will be only one object that is not *ruled out* by the description. Because the hearer knows that the speaker believes the *entire description,* he can then decide to believe the information conveyed by the additional descriptors is true of the single possibility that is not ruled out.

KAMP chooses a set of descriptors in the course of planning a DESCRIBE action to minimize both the number of descriptors chosen and the amount of effort required to plan the description. Choosing a provably minimal description requires an inordinate amount of effort and contributes nothing to the success of the action. KAMP chooses a set of descriptors by first selecting a *basic category* descriptor (Rosch et al., 1976) for the intended object and then adding descriptors from those facts about the object that are mutually known by both speaker and hearer, subject to the constraint that they are all linguistically realizable in the current noun phrase.

KAMP's description planning strategy and Axiom 6.5 are instantiations of the general Gricean maxim of quantity (Grice, 1975), which says "be neither more nor less informative than required." The Gricean principles are too vague as stated to be useful in a language planning system. However, frequently special cases of the principles manifest themselves in particular axioms and planning strategies. The minimal description strategy is one instance of the application of the maxim of quantity. The planner selects the shortest description that will convey the information necessary to identify its referent. The hearer assumes that a minimal description has been provided. When the description is richer than is necessary for referring, the hearer knows that other illocutionary intentions are involved.

The other action that can be used to realize the intention communication component of a concept activation action is *communicative pointing*. The following axiom describes pointing as another way of activating a concept.

$$(6.6) \quad \forall A, B, X, w_1, w_2 \, R(\mathrm{Do}(A, :\mathrm{Point}(B, X)), w_1, w_2) \supset$$
$$T(w_2, \mathbf{Mutually\text{-}Know}(@(A), @(B), \mathrm{Active}(@(X))))$$

Axiom 6.6 says that if an agent performs a pointing action, the standard name of the object he is pointing at becomes active.

A serious problem in formulating axioms such as 6.6 to characterize physical actions is deciding when they have communicative intent. In Figure 1.1 the expert is handing the apprentice the wheelpuller and intends this gesture to be interpreted with communicative intent as well. In a similar situation he may simply be grasping the tool for his own use and no communicative intentions are involved. The problem of deciding whether ordinary physical actions have communicative intent is deferred pending future research. Axiom 6.6 makes the simplifying assumption that any gestures of which the speaker and hearer are mutually aware have communicative intent, and all other physical actions are intended only for their physical effects.

6.8   Focusing and pronominalization

Focusing is a natural part of any communication process. When two agents participate in a dialogue, they share mutual knowledge about what is being discussed. These mutual beliefs can arise from general knowledge of the topic of the discourse

(Grosz, 1980), from the syntactic form of the utterance (Creider, 1979; Sidner, 1979), from the hearer's understanding of the speaker's intentions (Grosz et al., 1983), or from explicit linguistic cues such as *clue words* (Reichman, 1978) e.g., "anyway," "next," "then," and "OK."

Grosz describes two levels at which focusing phenomena occur: local and global. Global phenomena concern the organization of the discourse and its relation to the plans of the speaker and the hearer. Examples of these phenomena include the use of clue words to communicate to the hearer that the speaker intends to shift the discourse from one topic to another. In addition, the inferences about focusing drawn on the basis of the dialogue participants' shared knowledge about their plans falls under the global classification. Global focusing actions involve communicating the speaker's intentions about what is being discussed, and are therefore similar to illocutionary acts.

Local phenomena, on the other hand, concern individual utterances and the relationship between successive utterances. Local focusing phenomena have been called *immediate focusing* (Sidner, 1979) or *centering* (Grosz et al., 1983). Every discourse has a *backward-looking center*, C_b, (called the *immediate focus* by Sidner) and a set of *forward-looking centers*, C_f, (called *potential foci* by Sidner). Each utterance either maintains C_b at its previous value, reassigns C_b to a value chosen from C_f, or establishes entirely new values for C_b and C_f. When pronouns are used in a sentence, they are selected according to rules that govern the movement of C_b.

Grosz and Sidner have developed rules that describe the movement of C_b from sentence to sentence, and other rules that describe the dependence of pronominal anaphora on C_b and C_f. An example of such a rule is "For any discourse, if the last utterance was s_1 and the center was C_{b_1}, then, provided that the center of the next utterance s_2 is C_{b_2}, and $C_{b_2} = C_{b_1}$, then C_{b_2} must be referred to in a noun phrase of s_2 by a pronoun."

These two levels of focusing phenomena are different with respect to intention communication and are treated quite differently by the utterance planner. Global focusing is an intentional act. When a speaker wants to shift the topic of the discourse to something new, particularly when it is not clear that the hearer

119

should expect the topic to change, the speaker must communicate this intention by explicitly planning focusing actions.

Centering, on the other hand, is not necessarily an intentional action, but is a feature of communication that reduces the amount of mental processing necessary to produce and understand utterances. It is possible for speakers to intentionally violate conventions of centering under certain circumstances in an effort to induce a hearer to draw additional inferences, but this is relatively infrequent. Centering can be compared to breathing — a person can bring his breathing under conscious control, but most of the time he just breathes without being aware that it is happening and without making any conscious effort to do so.

KAMP is basically a single-utterance planner that does not reason about discourse per se. If KAMP generates more than one sentence, the sentences derive their coherence from being part of the same overall plan, rather than from being the realization of any discourse-level actions. The development of such discourse-level planning operators is an important area for future research. Until a good discourse planning theory is available, the planning of global focusing actions will not be dealt with. On the other hand, it is possible to axiomatize the local changes resulting from centering.

KAMP's axiomatization of centering is not discussed in detail in this book because it is still in a state of flux, and an adequate treatment of the phenomenon has yet to be developed. Currently, there is a term, C_b, whose denotation in each world is the center. It is assumed that the denotation of C_b is known to all participants at all times. A predicate C_f applies to all forward looking centers of the previous utterance. Currently C_f is the set of active concepts from the previous utterance. Choices of syntactic structure, such as topicalization and wh-clefts, have a strong influence on the center. Therefore, the axioms that describe center movement are stated as one of the effects of performing a surface speech act.

KAMP does not plan explicit center movements, but instead tries to keep the center as stable as possible. That implies that if any concept activated by the current utterance is the same as C_b, then KAMP plans to keep it as C_b by pronominalization and by specifying that the noun phrase activating C_b should appear as the surface subject. Whenever a concept in C_f is activated, KAMP pronominalizes it as long as the pronoun's features of number, gender, etc. distinguish the referent from C_b and other members of C_f. If the concept is not a member of C_f, or if pronominalization is impossible, then KAMP invokes the description planning mechanism outlined in the previous section.

6.9   Action subsumption

KAMP attempts to take advantage of opportunities to achieve multiple goals in a single utterance by recognizing situations in which *action subsumption* is possible. An important application of this principle is in the planning of referring expressions.

An action A_1 *subsumes* an action A_2 if A_1 and A_2 are part of the same plan, and also, (in addition to the effects for which it was planned), produces the effects for which A_2 was intended. Therefore, the resulting plan need only include action A_1 (and its expansion) to achieve all the goals.

The concept of action subsumption is particularly useful for planning linguistic actions because many options are normally available for expanding an illocutionary act into a surface speech act. The planner can frequently detect situations in which minor alterations of the expansion of an action will allow an action in another part of the plan to be subsumed. Although the term "minor alterations" is admittedly vague, the general idea is clear. When surface speech acts are being planned, it means making a change localized to one of the constituents of the sentence. Changes can be made to a surface speech act during the planning that do not alter the overall structure of the sentence, but are sufficient to subsume actions in the plan. An example of such a change is adding a descriptor to the description used in a referring expression by the inclusion of adjectives, prepositional phrases, and nonrestrictive relative clauses.

Action subsumption is related to what has been referred to in the planning literature as *opportunistic planning* (Hayes-Roth, 1979); this means designing a planner with a sufficiently flexible control structure to recognize and take advantage of various interactions among actions and goals. For example, if an agent has two goals, e.g., to eat bread and drink wine, an inefficient planner would go to the supermarket, buy bread, bring it home, go to the supermarket again, buy wine, and bring it home. An opportunistic planner would nótice that while the agent was at the supermarket, he would have the opportunity to satisfy the two goals simultaneously by buying both bread and wine on the same trip, thus optimizing his plan. Action subsumption is a special kind of opportunistic strategy focused on exploiting actions with multiple effects.

The principle on which action subsumption is based is to take maximum advantage of global interactions among actions in a plan. Such interactions are detected by the *critics* discussed in Section 4.3. The action subsumption critic works by first applying a set of rules to determine whether action subsumption might be possible. If so, it then tries several action subsumption strategies that specify the plan modification required. If a strategy is successful, the plan is altered accordingly and the subsumed action marked so that no further work will be done by the planner to expand it.

An example of action subsumption test rules would be to look for a situation in which an activation of a concept C is being performed, and where, in the same plan, there is a goal that the hearer knows that some property holds of C. The planner attempts to (1) expand the concept activation with a describe action, and (2) incorporate the property as one of the descriptors.

The critic must consider whether the subsuming noun phrase is being used to refer to its referent the first time, or if it corefers with another noun phrase in the discourse. Different constraints operate with coreferring noun phrases, as is illustrated by the following examples:

1. I told the guy at the door to watch out, but he wouldn't listen.

2. I told the guy at the door to watch out, but my brother wouldn't listen.

3. I told the guy at the door to watch out, but the bozo wouldn't listen.

Sentence (1) is perfectly acceptable, because the pronominal reference in the final clause conforms to the principle of pronominalizing the center. Sentence (2) violates the principal of referring to the center of the discourse without pronominalizing. Sentence (2) cannot be used to inform the hearer that the man at the door is the speaker's brother. Sentence (3), on the other hand, also violates the principle of pronominalizing the center, but the speaker may use this sentence successfully to convey his negative opinion of the person's intelligence. Evans (1981) asserts that all such uses of action subsumption must involve evaluative predicates. As the following pair of sentences seem to indicate, however, this does not appear to be correct:

1. My uncle took his dog to the vet yesterday.

2. The old Irish setter has been suffering from fleas for years.

Cohen (1981) has observed that the modality of the conversation affects the amount of action subsumption that people do when planning utterances. Action subsumption occurs more frequently in dialogues over teletype links than in face-to-face contact. It is speculated that either the bandwidth of teletype communication induces the planning of longer, more complex sentences, or the increased time available permits more complex planning to take place. KAMP makes no attempt to model processing constraints that affect human decisions as to whether to subsume actions, but this is certainly an interesting topic for research.

The possibility of action subsumption presents some minor difficulties for representing the relationship between illocutionary and surface speech acts in a prodedural network. When a surface speech act subsumes several illocutionary acts, it is reasonable to think of the performance of the act as executing several illocutionary acts in parallel. But, the KAMP formalism is not adapted to describing parallel actions. Treating the surface speech act as the expansion of one of the illocutionary acts, KAMP marks the other illocutionary acts as being *subsumed* by the surface speech act. The illocutionary act being subsumed is not expanded individually, and this is indicated by marking the action as a phantom in the network. Figure 6.6 illustrates the representation of a subsumed action in a procedural network.

Chapter 7 contains a detailed example of the planning of an utterance and describes how KAMP deals with the interaction between illocutionary acts and surface speech acts.

6.10   Planning indirect speech acts

Some utterances are intended by the speaker to have an illocutionary force other than that indicated by their literal meaning. Such utterances are called *indirect speech acts,* of which the following sentences are examples:

1. Do you want to play some backgammon?

2. It's two o'clock and I have to work.

Sentence (1) is a question in its surface form, but the speaker obviously intends for the hearer to recognize it as an invitation to actually play a game of backgammon. Sentence (2) is a refusal by the speaker to comply with the hearer's request, but, rather than simply saying no, the speaker informs the hearer of his reason for refusal. The hearer is expected to know that having to work precludes playing backgammon; consequently the statement is tantamount to a refusal. Searle (1979a) points out that indirect speech acts are intended literally, but the underlying illocutionary act entails the proposition expressed in the surface speech act. Thus, when the speaker asks, "Could you pass the salt?" it is acceptable for the speaker to answer the question literally (e.g., "Yes, here it is," or "No, I can't reach it.") as long as the intention to make a request is recognized. Clark (1979) has performed experiments that seem to indicate that speakers do process

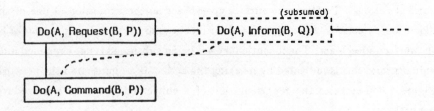

Figure 6.6:   A subsumed surface speech act in a procedural net

and respond to the surface form of indirect requests in addition to recognizing the intentions that underlie them.

Some types of indirect speech acts have become highly conventionalized. It is plausible to assume that such ubiquitous modal questions as "Could you get me a glass of water?" are planned without recourse to the general reasoning mechanism that would be required to understand "It's awfully cold in here" as a request to close a window. Syntactic evidence supports this distinction as well, since "please" can be used with conventional indirect requests as in "Could you please get me a glass of water?" but not with unconventional requests.

KAMP does not currently plan indirect speech acts. To do this adequately would require the solution of several very difficult problems. First, it is necessary to characterize the reasons for planning indirect requests, so a planner would have some basis for choosing an indirect act instead of a direct one. These reasons invariably involve the satisfaction of multiple goals. For example, indirect requests are frequently planned to satisfy goals relating to politeness, a concept that is notoriously difficult to formalize. Lakoff (1973) describes some cross-cultural maxims for politeness such as "leave options" and "don't impose." These vague criteria need to be defined with sufficient precision to make a formal treatment possible.

It is conceivable that a planner that plans only conventional indirect speech acts could have enough knowledge built into it to enable it to use a theory of politeness for planning indirect requests. However, if the planner were designed to plan unconventional indirect speech acts as well, the surface speech act axioms would have to be extended to describe the conditions under which a hearer would interpret the surface speech act as one illocutionary act as opposed to another.

Searle (1979a) lists some rules about how speakers can perform indirect commissives. For example, one rule is that "[a speaker] can make an indirect commissive by either asking whether or stating that a preparatory condition concerning his ability to do [an action] obtains." Therefore, "I can come tomorrow," can be understood as a promise that the speaker will be at a meeting the next day. Brown (1979) has extended these rules to a variety of speech acts, including requesting and informing, and has used these rules as the basis of a system for recognizing and interpreting indirect speech acts. Rules such as these need to be incorporated into axioms similar to Axiom 6.1. The problem with this approach is that it requires anticipating all the possible indirect uses of a surface speech act. The sheer number of alternatives compiled by Brown suggests that this is a difficult task; furthermore there is always the possibility that a speech act could be used in a novel indirect way that is not covered by the rules. If more were understood about why unconventional indirect speech acts are employed in certain situations, a more general approach might be possible.

6.11   Conclusion

This chapter has examined several issues pertaining to the planning of surface linguistic acts. It has always been stressed in this research that utterances are multifaceted actions that produce many kinds of effects simultaneously. A single utterance can inform the hearer of several propositions, make a request, change shared beliefs about the topic of the discourse, and convey the speaker's social assessment of the hearer. The utterance planner's task is to plan actions that satisfy these diverse goals and then implement these high-level actions as utterances (and perhaps physical actions as well) in the most efficient manner possible. This may require making decisions about whether illocutionary acts are best realized directly or indirectly.

This chapter has discussed how the KAMP system integrates planning knowledge and linguistic knowledge through the TELEGRAM grammar and how it employs action subsumption to construct utterances that satisfy multiple goals. This requires the axiomatization of a great diversity of action types: surface speech acts, concept activation actions, focusing, and centering. In addition, a means of coordinating physical and linguistic actions has been described that enables the planning of pointing actions to communicate the intention to refer.

Since so many different actions can be performed and intentions communicated by a single utterance, each of these actions and intentions must be examined and a rigorous formal theory of them developed if the feasibility of an utterance planner is to be demonstrated. In this initial study, breadth has been emphasized at the expense of depth; hence a fairly large number of problems, while touched upon, remain as topics for future research. Some of these possibilities are discussed in greater depth in Chapter 8. In essence, however, the framework developed here appears to be a promising vehicle of research in the continuing effort to increase our understanding of communication.

7
Utterance planning: an example

7.1 Introduction

This chapter discusses in detail a typical example that requires KAMP to form a plan involving several physical and illocutionary acts, and then to integrate the illocutionary acts into a single utterance. This example does not reflect every aspect of utterance planning, but hopefully touches upon enough of them to enable an understanding of the way KAMP works, to illustrate the principles discussed in earlier chapters of this book, and to provide a demonstration of KAMP's power and some of its limitations. It is important to bear in mind that the implementation of KAMP was done to test the *feasability* of a particular approach to multiagent planning and language generation. Since it is not intended to be a "production" system, many details of efficiency involving both fundamental issues and engineering problems have been purposely disregarded in this discussion.

KAMP is based on a first-order logic natural-deduction system[9] that is similar in many respects to the one proposed by Moore (1980). The current implementation does not take advantage of well-known techniques such as structure sharing and indexing that could be used to reduce some of the computational effort required. Nevertheless, the system is reliable, albeit inefficient, in making the necessary deductions to solve problems similar to the one described here.

Without apologizing further for the implementation's inadequacies, it is obvious that the computational effort required to produce a single utterance almost certainly precludes the practical application of KAMP's problem solving approach to language generation in the near future. However, the theoretical ideas are important, since it is apparent from the examination of dialogues that reasoning processes similar to those modeled by KAMP must be followed by speakers when they produce utterances. It is clear from the research behind KAMP that modeling these reasoning processes requires a great deal of computational power, given the deduction system currently employed. It remains a topic for future research to determine how the ideas discussed in this book can be applied at reasonable cost.

7.2   The problem and the domain

KAMP's initial domain comprises the assembly and repair of a complex electrome-chanical device. The user of the system is a novice seeking assistance. This is an ideal domain for several reasons. Dialogue protocols have been collected (Deutsch, 1975) that constitute a body of linguistic data raising interesting issues and fur-nishing examples of phenomena that are explainable by the theory on which KAMP is based. The two agents involved have different levels of domain knowledge and different physical capabilities — an environment that engenders a natural need for communication. To reduce the scope of the problem, the only illocutionary acts considered are informing and requesting, while the only referring actions allowed are those that are based on mutual knowledge. Another advantage of this domain is that, subject to these restrictions, it is still possible to carry on a reasonable dialogue.

Figure 7.1 illustrates a typical situation in which KAMP operates. This domain has two agents called Rob and John. Rob is a "robot" that incorporates KAMP for planning and deduction. Rob's only connection with the world is the computer terminal, so, though capable of performing speech acts, he cannot perform any actions that affect the physical state of the world directly. John is assumed to be a person capable of performing both speech acts and physical actions. The particular situation for this example includes a piece of equipment to be repaired (in this case an air compressor) and some tools that are necessary for the task. The tools can be out in plain view on the table, in which case Rob and John mutually know their location and other observable physical properties, or they can be stored away out of sight in the toolbox, in which case Rob may know where they are, but not necessarily John. In general, Rob is the expert and he knows almost everything about the situation. For example, Rob knows how to assemble the compressor because he knows how the parts fit together, he knows what tools to use for the various assembly operations, and he knows where all the tools are located.

This domain provides an ideal setting for studying multiagent planning as it relates to the production of utterances. Communication arises naturally in this domain because of the disparity in knowledge and capabilities of the agents. Since Rob is incapable of performing physical actions, he must make requests of John whenever he wants to change the physical state of the world. Since Rob knows all there is to know about the task, and John knows this, John must therefore ask questions to get the information he needs to do a task; by the same token, Rob must provide John with the information he knows he needs when he requests John

Figure 7.1: KAMP's Domain

to do something. Thus, the need for communication arises for either agent to be able to satisfy his goals.

Part of the description of the domain includes an axiomatization of the possible actions that can be carried out by the agents and the corresponding KAMP action summaries. The initial state of the physical world, as well as each agent's knowledge about the world, must be described.

The following assertions describe the initial state of the world in the example under consideration (the symbols John, Rob, PU, PL, T1, TB1, WR1, B1, LOC1 and LOC2 are all rigid designators):

(7.1)	$\Box$ (Human(John))
(7.2)	$\Box$ (Robot(Rob))
(7.3)	$\Box$ (Pump(PU))
(7.4)	$\Box$ (Platform(PL))
(7.5)	$\Box$ (Table(T1))
(7.6)	$\Box$ (Tool-box(TB1))
(7.7)	$\Box$ (Wrench(WR1))
(7.8)	$\Box$ (Bolt(B1))
(7.9)	$\Box$ (Workbench(WB1))
(7.10)	$\Box$ (**Knowref**(Rob, Location(John)))
(7.11)	$\Box$ (**Knowref**(John, Location(Rob)))
(7.12)	$\Box$ ($\forall x$ Wrench(x) $\supset$ Tool(x))
(7.13)	$\Box$ ($\forall x$ Human(x) $\vee$ Robot(x) $\supset$ Animate(x))
(7.14)	$\Box$ ($\forall x, y, z$ Pump(x) $\wedge$ Attached(x, y) $\wedge$ Attached(x, z) $\supset y = z$)
(7.15)	$\Box$ ($\forall x$ Animate(x) $\supset$ **Knowref**(x, Location(x)))

Note that, since Axioms 7.1–7.15 are *necessarily* true (i.e., true in all possible worlds), they are universally known. It may seem implausible that the facts expressed by Axioms 7.10 and 7.11 should be treated as necessarily true, but the assumption that Rob and John always mutually know each other's location simplifies the example sufficiently to enable us to make the assumption despite its apparent implausibility.

The following facts are true of the initial state of the world, but, because they change over time, are not necessarily true.

(7.16)   **True**(Location(John) = Location(WB1))
(7.17)   **True**(Location(Rob) = Location(WB1))

John and Rob are both initially at the workbench. The "Location" predicate is used very loosely, meaning roughly that it is close enough to enable the execution of actions directly affecting the object. Any attempt to be more detailed than this would lead us astray into the thorny problems of spatial reasoning.

The following assertions describe the mutual knowledge of the agents:

(7.18)   **True**(**Mutually-Know**(John, Rob, Attached(PU, PL)))
(7.19)   □ (Fastener(B1, PU, PL))
(7.20)   **True**(**Mutually-Know**(John, Rob, Fastened(B1, PU, PL)))
(7.21)   **True**(**Mutually-Know**(John, Rob, Location(PL) = Location(WB1)))

Axiom 7.18 says that John and Rob mutually know that the pump is initially attached to the platform, Axioms 7.19 and 7.20 say that bolt B1 is the fastener used to attach the pump to the platform and that, in the initial state, it is fastened; finally, Axiom 7.21 says that Rob and John mutually know that the platform is on the workbench.

The example also requires some axioms that describe the instrument relation:

(7.22) $\forall x, y, z, i$ Fastener$(z, x) \wedge ($Tool$(z) = i) \supset$ Instrument(Unfasten$(x, y, z, i))$
(7.23) $\forall x, y, z, i$ Instrument(Unfasten$(x, y, z, i)) \supset$ Instrument(Remove$(x, y, i))$

Axiom 7.23 says that the instrument of an unfastening action is also the instrument of a removing action, which is natural, since unfastening is part of the process of removal. Axiom 7.22 says that, if z is some fastener (e.g., a bolt) that attaches x to something, and i is an appropriate tool for manipulating it (e.g., a wrench), then i is an instrument for any action of unfastening x from whatever it is attached to.

To plan a description successfully, some knowledge is needed to limit the number of objects to which a predicate applies, thereby guaranteeing the ability to prove that a conjunction of descriptors identifies a single object. The most general way to do this is with a circumscription schema (McCarthy, 1980); however for the sake of simplicity in this example, we shall content ourselves with explicit assertions about the uniqueness of the objects.

(7.24)   **True(Mutually-Know**(John, Rob, $\forall x$ Wrench$(x) \supset x =$ WR1))

(7.25)   **True(Mutually-Know**(John, Rob, $\forall x$ Pump$(x) \supset x =$ PU))

(7.26)   **True(Mutually-Know**(John, Rob, $\forall x$ Tool-box$(x) \supset x =$ TB1))

The set domain-specific axioms is completed by axioms that describe the knowledge of agents that is *not* shared by them. In this case, we shall assume that Rob knows that the tool for removing the bolt is the wrench WR1, that it is located in the toolbox, and that this knowledge is not necessarily shared by John. These facts are expressed in axioms 7.27 and 7.28.

(7.27)   **True(Know**(Rob, Tool(B1) = WR1))

(7.28)   **True(Know**(Rob, Location(WR1) = Location(TB1)))

The axioms for illocutionary acts have been described in Chapter 5. Chapter 6 discussed axioms for surface speech acts and focusing, while Chapter 4 presented a plan involving the action of moving. The domain-specific actions of unfastening and removing are straightforward physical actions and will not be included here. The only deviation from the example of physical actions like MOVE discussed in chapter 4 is that the preconditions of physical actions are augmented by the assertion that they can be performed only by a human, whereas the agent of a speech act can be any animate object.

The following notation is used for the illustrations in this chapter. Each node in the plan has a boldface label (**P1**, **P2**, etc.) to make it easier to refer to. Dotted boxes are used to represent phantom goals. The successor relationship between actions is represented by solid connecting lines, hierarchical relationships by dotted lines. Each node has an associated world. For goal nodes, the world is written inside parentheses (e.g., (W_i)), to represent the notion that the planner is to start in world W_i and formulate actions designed to attain a world in which the goal will be satisfied. For phantom nodes, the world name is not in parentheses; this means that the goal is actually satisfied within the indicated world. Action nodes have a label such as "$W_i \rightarrow W_j$" to identify the action as a transformation relating worlds W_i and W_j.

Actions will often be planned without knowing precisely what worlds they will be performed in, or precisely what world will result from the action. This is particularly true of actions that are represented at a high level of abstraction. Worlds are represented in the diagram as "?" if, at that point, the planner has not yet assigned a definite world. (Note that KAMP can often reason about what is true at a given point in the plan, even though it has not assigned a world to the node, since frame axioms can be stated for high-level actions that describe some changes and leave others unspecified.) A notation such as "$W_i \rightarrow$?" labels a high-level action that may be expanded to several actions at a lower level. The planner knows that the action sequence will begin in W_1 but it will not know the resulting world until expansion of the action has taken place. A notation such as "? $\rightarrow$?" is used when the planner knows where in a sequence a high-level action must occur in relation to other actions in the plan, but it cannot assign either an initial or a final world.

7.3   Details of the grammar

To avoid burdening the reader with unnecessary detail, the TELEGRAM grammar will not be described in its entirety here, but rather only those parts that play a direct role in the unifications required by this example.

As described in Chapter 6, the grammar consists of a set of alternatives, each corresponding to a major lexical category or type of constituent. The alternative corresponding to imperative sentences is shown in Figure 7.2. The imperative has a null subject, a verb corresponding to the predicate, a noun phrase referring to

$$
\begin{bmatrix}
\text{MOOD} = \text{IMPERATIVE} \\
\text{PAT} = (\ldots < \text{VG} >< \text{OBJ} >< \text{ADVPP} > \ldots) \\
\text{SUBJ} = \text{NONE} \\
< \text{VG VERB} > = \begin{bmatrix} \text{CAT} = \text{V} \\ \text{PRED} = < \uparrow \text{PRED} > \end{bmatrix} \\
\text{OBJ} = \begin{bmatrix} \text{CAT} = \text{NP} \\ \text{REFERENT} = < \uparrow \text{GOAL} > \end{bmatrix}
\end{bmatrix}
$$

Figure 7.2:   Grammatical description of imperative sentence

the goal argument, and possibly an adverbial prepositional phrase.

The basic propositional content of a sentence is represented by a predicate and its associated arguments, identified by their case role. TELEGRAM specifies how the case roles are mapped onto syntactic constituents.

The structure of adverbial prepositional phrases is given by the fragment of the grammar in Figure 7.3. The FD specifies a prepositional phrase with a preposition that can convey a particular kind of relationship (represented by the PRED feature) between the event described by the sentence and the denotation of the object of the prepositional phrase (the REFERENT of the OBJ feature).

The lexicon is assumed to contain a set of words identified by their category and their semantics. For example, the verb *"remove"* is entered in the lexicon as

$$\begin{bmatrix} \text{CAT} = \text{V} \\ \text{LEX} = \text{``remove''} \\ \text{SUBCAT} = \text{TRANS} \\ \text{PRED} = \text{REMOVE} \end{bmatrix}$$

and the preposition *"with"* is represented as

$$\begin{bmatrix} \text{CAT} = \text{P} \\ \text{LEX} = \text{``with''} \\ \left\{ \begin{array}{l} \text{PRED} = \text{INSTRUMENT} \\ \text{PRED} = \text{POSSESS} \\ \text{PRED} = \text{ACCOMPANY} \\ \qquad \vdots \end{array} \right\} \end{bmatrix}$$

$$\begin{bmatrix} \text{CAT} = \text{ADVPP} \\ \text{PAT} = (\ldots < \text{PP} > \ldots) \\ \text{PRED} = \text{INSTRUMENT} \\ \text{PP} = \begin{bmatrix} \text{CAT} = \text{PP} \\ \text{PREP} = \begin{bmatrix} \text{CAT} = \text{P} \\ \text{PRED} = <\uparrow \text{PRED}> \end{bmatrix} \\ \text{OBJ} = \begin{bmatrix} \text{CAT} = \text{NP} \\ \text{REFERENT} = <\uparrow \text{ARG}> \end{bmatrix} \end{bmatrix} \end{bmatrix}$$

Figure 7.3: Functional description of an adverbial prepositional phrase

7.4   Planning the utterance

The top-level goal that is given to Rob (and thus to KAMP) is

$$\textbf{True}(\neg\text{Attached}(\text{PU}, \text{PL})).$$

It is also necessary to tell KAMP which agent is doing the planning. If it knows that Rob is doing the planning, it can assume that Rob will want to carry out any action that satisfies a goal, while this condition must be verified explicitly for any agent other than Rob (see Chapter 4).

The first thing KAMP does is create a procedural network from the goal. This initial goal is depicted as node P1 in Figure 7.4. Once the initial procedural network is created, KAMP proceeds as outlined in Chapter 4 to expand the initial goal node into a plan. As you will recall, KAMP proceeds in a series of cycles in which each goal node and high-level action is expanded. Then critics examine the plan, making modifications based on the detection of global interactions. Finally, after criticism, the FD associated with each surface speech act is unified with the TELEGRAM grammar.

The actions in KAMP's domain are divided into three levels of abstraction: the high-level actions are the illocutionary acts and the physical action of removing; the next level consists of surface speech acts and concept activation actions; the lowest level consists of description planning, the uttering of sentences, unfastening, grasping, and moving. When KAMP has performed the number of expansion-criticism cycles needed to expand the entire plan fully to the next lower level of abstraction, it verifies that the plan works by proving that the top-level goal is true in the world resulting from the planned actions.

Let us now return to the example. After KAMP has created the initial network, it tries to show that Rob knows the goal is satisfied in the current state of the

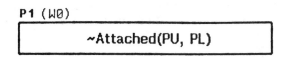

P1 (W0)

~Attached(PU, PL)

Figure 7.4:   The initial procedural network

world, W_0. Since the goal is not satisfied, however, further planning is required, which results in the procedural network depicted in Figure 7.5. KAMP consults the action summaries to determine whether there is any action it knows about at this level of abstraction that achieves the goal as one of its effects. The action of removing has the desired effect, but the action preconditions specify that only humans can perform removing actions; since Rob is a nonhuman animate, KAMP plans to achieve the goal by having John remove the pump (creating node **P4** of Figure 7.5). To have John remove the pump, KAMP must also establish two preconditions: that John *intend* to remove the pump (node **P2**) and that John be in the same place as the pump (node **P3**). Because the latter is already satisfied, it is marked as a phantom, and attention is focused on **P2**.

In the next expansion-criticism cycle of the highest abstraction level, KAMP tries to show that John wants to remove the pump in world W_0. Since there is no knowledge to support that conclusion, KAMP follows its procedure of checking action summaries and selecting an action that is likely to achieve the goal. The action summaries indicate that the REQUEST action has the intended effect, so KAMP plans for Rob to request of John that he remove the pump. This leads KAMP to construct the procedural net represented in Figure 7.6. A complete plan has now been formulated at the highest level of abstraction. No critics apply to the plan at this level, therefore, KAMP then attempts to prove that the plan it has proposed so far actually works. Given Axioms 7.1–7.23 together with axioms for REMOVE, the verification step succeeds, and KAMP proceeds down to the next

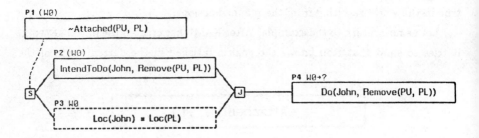

Figure 7.5: Rob plans for John to remove the pump

level in the abstraction hierarchy.

Surface speech acts are introduced into the plan at this lower level, which entails the inclusion of actual utterances in the plan. KAMP must reason about what surface speech acts will be interpreted by the hearer as equivalent to the REQUEST in node **P6**. It is at this point that the opportunity for multiple-goal satisfaction through the planning of an indirect speech act would be considered. However, as discussed in Section 6.10, KAMP plans to implement the REQUEST directly as a COMMAND (node **P7** of Figure 7.7).

KAMP must encode the propositional content of the surface speech act, expressed in a standard logical notation in which the role of each argument is identified by its position, into a functional description in which each argument to the predicate is the value of some feature. The features to which the arguments of the propositional content are assigned are the various case roles specified by the grammar. KAMP reasons at this time about whether the hearer can infer any of the arguments to the proposition. In this example, the hearer knows (Axiom 7.14) that the pump can be attached to only one thing, and that it is attached to the platform, PL (Axiom 7.18). Consequently, if he knows he must remove the pump, he knows that it is the platform he must remove it from, thus making it

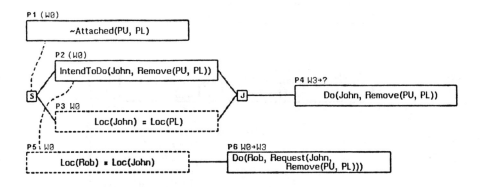

Figure 7.6:   Rob requests that John remove the pump

unnecessary to specify the argument PL in the FD of the command. Figure 7.7 shows the expansion of the REQUEST and illustrates the corresponding functional description associated with the COMMAND.

Since the request is the only illocutionary act planned so far, there is no more linguistic planning to be done at this stage. The functional description is ready to be unified with the grammar, but this unification does not take place until the entire plan has been expanded to the same level of abstraction as the surface speech act. This entails expansion of the REMOVE node as well. Since REMOVE is a physical action, KAMP proceeds exactly as outlined in Chapter 4. Removing something requires that each of the fasteners that attach it be removed from whatever it is connected to. In the present case, it requires removing the bolt B1, since Axioms 7.19 and 7.20 state that B1 fastens PU to PL. To undo a fastener, some sort of tool appropriate for the particular fastener must be employed. At this point the plan is formed by using the intensional description, Tool(B1), meaning something like "the tool for removing B1." The action-specific and universal preconditions for unfastening are inserted into the plan, thereby yielding the procedural net of Figure 7.8. The precondition nodes are **P8**, **P9** and **P10** — that John must know what the tool is, that John must be in the same place as the

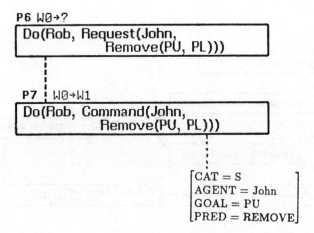

Figure 7.7: A request expanded as an imperative sentence

140

platform, and that John must have the tool.

In the world resulting from the performance of the REQUEST in node **P6**, KAMP knows that John is already in the same location as PL, and therefore the goal **P9** is a phantom. Rob does not know whether John has the tool, nor does Rob even know that John knows what the tool is. Therefore, KAMP plans for Rob to inform John that the tool for removing bolt B1 is wrench WR1 (node **P14** in Figure 7.9).

The critics are again applied to the plan, but at this stage of development, none of the critics apply. After the cycle of expansion and criticism has been completed, KAMP finds each functional description associated with a surface speech-act node and unifies it with the grammar. The unification of the FD of Figure 7.7 with the portion of the grammar FD shown in Figure 7.2 results in the FD depicted in Figure 7.10. For each feature whose value appears in the pattern contained within the PAT feature, that FD is recursively unified with the grammar. That means that the VG and OBJ features of the FD in Figure 7.10 will be unified. Unification of the VG feature results eventually in the selection of a verb from the lexicon with the right syntactic and semantic properties, i.e., with a set of features that unify with the value of the VERB feature. In this case the chosen verb is *remove*. When

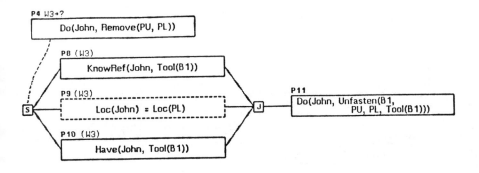

Figure 7.8: KAMP's plan for John to remove the pump

Planning English sentences

the value of the OBJ feature is unified with the grammar, the unifier will attempt
to match the REFERENT feature with a feature in the grammar, but will fail.
As described in Chapter 6, information attached to the feature name REFERENT
tells the planner to create a goal that the object of the referent feature will be an
active concept, (node **P15** of Figure 7.11) and to give control back to the planner
to decide on the best means of accomplishing that goal.

KAMP knows that performing a DESCRIBE action to achieve the activation
of a concept is justified by Axiom 6.5. In this case, PU is the only object mutually known to the speaker and hearer that can be described as a pump, so the
description $\lambda x\,(\text{Pump}(x))$ is chosen as a description for the referring expression,
thus achieving the intention communication goal. The linguistic realization of the
action consists in augmenting the functional description of the sentence with appropriate features to reflect the choice of the description. KAMP uses a simple
and not particularly interesting method of associating predicates with features
by means of property lists, thus ignoring many problems of lexical choice for the

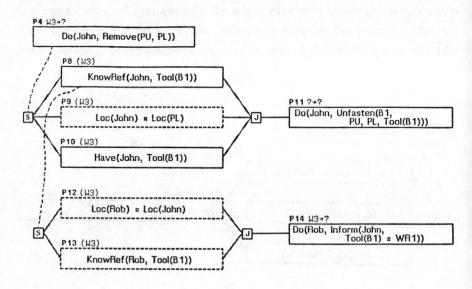

Figure 7.9: John needs to know what the tool is, so Rob tells him

142

sake of simplification. The property list of the predicate "Pump" suggests using the noun *pump*. The describe action specifies the insertion of the DESCRIPTION feature into the FD of figure 7.10, and further unification specifies the head noun.

Since one more round of expansion has taken place, namely the planning of the concept activation of PU and its associated description, the critics are again invoked. As explained in Chapter 4, each critic has a simple test that it applies to the plan to verify its applicability. The action-subsumption critic's test works by examining pairs of illocutionary acts, such as the newly introduced informing action **P14** of Figure 7.9 and the request **P6** of Figure 7.7, to see if there is a relationship between the two actions that can be exploited for the purpose of action subsumption, as described in Chapter 6. The situation most frequently exploited by the action subsumption critic is one in which the speaker informs the hearer about the property of some individual who is also the object of a concept activation action associated with some other surface speech act in the plan. If there is no surface speech act that activates the concept, the propositional content of one of the surface speech acts can then perhaps (grammatical constraints permitting) be modified to enable the planning of a concept activation action that subsumes the informing action. That is the case with node **P14** of this example.

The action subsumption critic can use Axioms 7.23 and 7.27 to prove that the

$$
\begin{bmatrix}
\text{CAT} = \text{S} \\
\text{PAT} = (\ldots < \text{VG} >< \text{OBJ} > \ldots) \\
\text{GOAL} = \text{PU} \\
\text{AGENT} = \text{John} \\
\text{SUBJ} = \text{NONE} \\
\text{OBJ} = \begin{bmatrix} \text{CAT} = \text{NP} \\ \text{REFERENT} = \text{PU} \\ \text{DESCRIPTION} = \lambda x(\text{Pump}(x)) \\ \text{HEAD} = \begin{bmatrix} \text{CAT} = \text{N} \\ \text{PRED} = \text{Pump} \end{bmatrix} \end{bmatrix} \\
\text{PRED} = \text{REMOVE} \\
\text{VG} = \begin{bmatrix} \text{VERB} = \begin{bmatrix} \text{CAT} = \text{V} \\ \text{PRED} = \text{REMOVE} \end{bmatrix} \end{bmatrix}
\end{bmatrix}
$$

Figure 7.10: The partial result of unification of the COMMAND FD

action of **P14** is actually informing the hearer of an instrument relation between the removal action and the tool being used to unfasten the bolt. The INFORM can be subsumed by the request if the instrumentality is explicitly predicated by an adverbial prepositional phrase in the request.

The action subsumption critic must determine whether all the preconditions for the subsumption candidate will also be satisfied in the state of the world when the subsuming action is performed. All the conditions, namely, that Rob is in the same location as John and that Rob knows that $Tool(B1) = WR1$, are satisfied in this situation. The action subsumption critic does two things: it moves the INFORM node to a position in the network immediately following the REQUEST; it modifies the functional description attached to the COMMAND node to include a feature describing the adverbial prepositional phrase. Figure 7.11 illustrates the effect of this subsumption on the part of the plan that concerns the expansion of

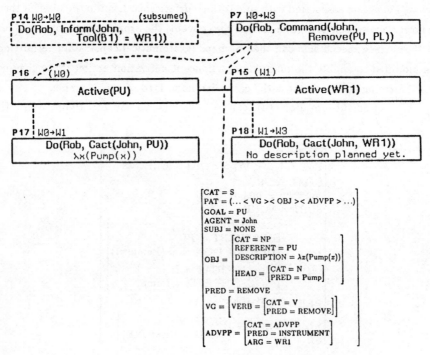

Figure 7.11: Subsuming the informing action

144

the request in **P6**.

The expansion of REMOVE is discarded and replanned because the hearer's knowledge has changed. This change stems from the fact that he will have been informed at this stage of the plan that the tool for removing the bolt is the wrench — a difference in knowledge that can cause a corresponding difference in the expansion of the REMOVE. Since there is no quick way to determine exactly what effect this will have on the plan, the entire portion of the plan developed under the previous assumption is discarded and reformulated. The result of the second expansion is illustrated in Figure 7.12.

Through an analysis of the discarded actions and the interaction of their effects, it may be possible to reduce computational effort by avoiding the total

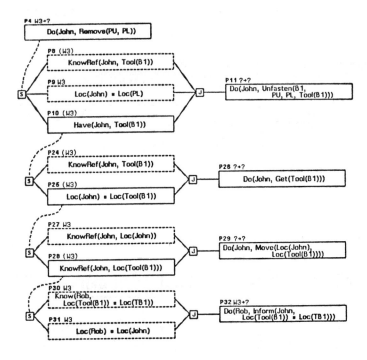

Figure 7.12: Expanding the REMOVE action after subsumption

replanning of portions of the plan. This is an example of the kind of efficiency factors that were ignored during the implementation of KAMP, and to some degree explains the slowness of the system.

Having done another round of expansion, the planner criticizes the plan. The action subsumption critic now realizes there is a situation similar to the one with informing action **P16**. The new informing action (represented as node **P17** in Figure 7.12) is a candidate for subsumption by the request because it informs the hearer of a property of an object whose concept is being activated as part of another utterance. As in the previous case, the INFORM is relocated so that it follows the REQUEST, the propositional content of the INFORM is made part of the description that activates WR1, and, as was done before, the part of the plan that may be affected by the hearer's new knowledge is discarded and replanned. Figure 7.13 depicts the expansion of the request after this last round of criticism.

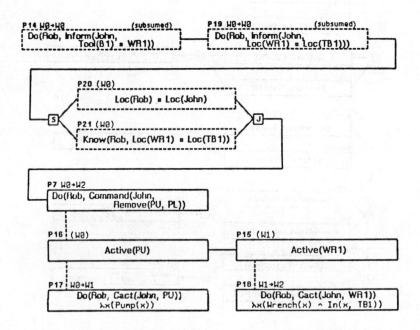

Figure 7.13: The second INFORM action subsumed

The unification is continued with the FD augmented by the features contributed by the description added for action subsumption. There are no more features that trigger activation of the planner, and all other features added to the FD during unification specify syntactic details such as subject-verb agreement, which have no significance for intention communication.

When the REMOVE action is expanded for the third time, the goals involving John's knowledge (**P10, P18, P21** and **P22** of Figure 7.14) are marked as phantoms. On the next criticism pass, the resolve-conflicts critic will notice that the action of John's moving to the toolbox to get the wrench undoes the phantom goal that places John at the platform so he can remove the pump. The conflict resolution critic proposes linearization of the split so that the goal of John being at the platform is achieved after he goes to the tool box and gets the wrench. Figure 7.14 shows the plan after the criticism by the conflict resolution critic and the expansion of the goal of John's being at the platform into the MOVE action, **P23**.

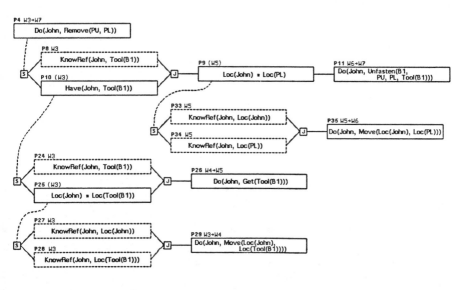

Figure 7.14: The final plan to remove the pump

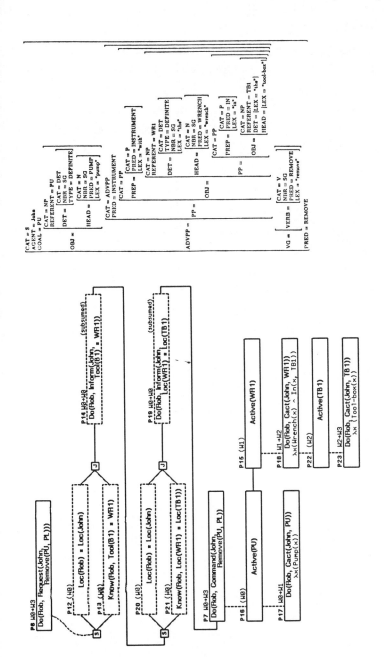

Figure 7.15: The final utterance plan

7.5   Conclusion

This chapter, by examining a single example in detail, has described how KAMP plans utterances. Of course, this is just one instance of a large class of situations in which KAMP is capable of performing.

KAMP does not currently have a very large or sophisticated grammar, since most of the effort devoted to it has been directed toward bridging the gap between abstractly specified illocutionary acts and surface English sentences. For this reason, most of the problems of lexical choice, representation of grammatical knowledge, and reasoning about social goals have been reserved for future research.

KAMP is designed to perform well in planning illocutionary acts that satisfy a speaker's goals involving the knowledge and intentions of other agents. KAMP can then examine the plan that contains illocutionary acts and can plan appropriate utterances to realize them by using such action subsumption strategies as adding modifiers to noun phrases to achieve multiple goals in a single utterance. KAMP is also capable of reasoning about how a speaker's physical actions affect the hearer's knowledge of the speaker's intentions.

It is clear from the experience gathered during the implementation of KAMP that the problem-solving techniques described here indeed do constitute a feasible approach to producing utterances that satisfy multiple goals. Although many practical engineering problems remain to be resolved, this work represents the first step in that direction.

8

Utterance planning: the future

8.1 What has been accomplished

KAMP represents the first step in a very ambitious program of research. It is appropriate at this time to reflect upon this program, how far we have come, and what lies in the future.

KAMP represents not merely an attempt to devise an expedient strategy for getting text out of a computer, but rather embodies an entire theory of communication. The goal of such a theory could be summarized by saying that its objective is to account for how agents manage to intentionally affect the beliefs, desires and intentions of other agents. Developing such a theory requires examining utterances to determine the goals the speakers are attempting to achieve thereby, and in the process explicating the knowledge about their environment, about their audience, and about their language that these speakers must have. Language generation has been chosen as an ideal vehicle for the study of problems arising from such a theory because it requires one to face the problem of why speakers choose to do the things they do in a way that is not required by language understanding. Theories of language understanding make heavy use of the fact that the speaker is behaving according to a coherent plan. Language generation requires producing such a coherent plan in the first place, and therefore requires uncovering the underlying principles that make such a plan coherent.

The goal of building a general theory of communication has significantly influenced the methodology of the research. If the ultimate goal was merely to produce grammatical sentences given their logical form, any one of a number of approaches could have resulted in a system that produces them quickly and efficiently. This is not to deny that such systems have useful applications, or to claim that they do not address interesting research issues in their own right. Such projects would simply fail to give us the insights into the general problem of communication that can be gained by the approach outlined in this book.

The primary advances that the research on KAMP has provided are a theory of speech acts that separates the action being performed from the sentence in a way that can account for the satisfaction of multiple goals in a single utterance, an integration of various kinds of communicative acts within a single framework, and a general design framework for an utterance planning system.

The axioms for linguistic actions are the most important components of KAMP, because they provide the formal description of the different kinds of actions that KAMP is capable of planning. The axioms for illocutionary acts are similar to those of previous systems (Cohen and Perrault, 1979) that describe the effects of speech acts in terms of the hearer's recognition of the speaker's intention to perform the act. The significant new contribution of the KAMP theory is an axiomatization of surface speech acts and concept activation actions that relates these actions to the illocutionary acts. The crucial motivation behind this step is to axiomatize the process by which a single sentence can be used by a speaker to perform several actions simultaneously, thereby satisfying multiple goals.

Another important advance represented by KAMP is allowing for integrated planning of physical and linguistic actions. This is significant for two reasons. First, in an environment in which cooperation with other agents is necessary, a need for communication inevitably arises. Therefore, plans will include both communicative acts and actions that are intended to accomplish physical-state goals. Frequently physical actions as well as linguistic actions will arise from the need to perform communicative acts. These actions may simply achieve enabling conditions such as moving the speaker closer to the hearer so his utterance is intelligible, or the physical actions may have communicative content in their own right, such as gestures. Second, there are strong interactions between the physical and linguistic actions that comprise a coherent plan. Gestures are not linguistic acts, however they may be planned in response to alternatives or lack thereof that the grammar provides for constructing referring expressions. Similarly, the performance of a gesture has an effect on which linguistic alternatives are chosen in the course of planning the utterance. The need to reason about and coordinate physical and linguistic actions argues strongly in favor of an integrated system such as KAMP.

Finally, KAMP illustrates the architecture of an utterance planning system that can serve as the basis for future research in this area. The division of actions into levels of abstraction is crucial to the logical separation of communicative acts from the utterances that realize them. The ability to examine a plan and take advantage of interactions of actions opportunistically is an important feature of KAMP's design. Although alternative designs for an utterance planner are conceiveable, these features are crucial to such a system regardless of the modularization of its components or the philosophy behind its knowledge representation system. The integration of linguistic knowledge and planning knowledge by means of the unification algorithm and the TELEGRAM grammar is also an important contribution. KAMP is evidence that a general planning mechanism, suitably modified, is a feasible design for a system that plans communicative acts and generates sentences. Although many problems remain to be solved, the basic system design will provide a foundation from which future research can proceed.

8.2 What remains to be done

A wise man once said, "The more I learn, the more I realize my ignorance." Certainly one of the most important contributions of any significant research effort is the uncovering of problems for future research and the definition of them in a way that permits rapid progress. KAMP has been no exception in this regard. Throughout this book, there have been numerous statements of the form "... but this problem will be deferred for future research." This section summarizes the most important of these problems that are particularly relevant to the research on KAMP.

8.2.1 *Relationship between action hierarchy levels*

One major area for research is the formalization of the relationship among actions in the abstraction hierarchy. The approach taken by KAMP, following

Searle (1969), assumes a speech act communicates the speaker's intentions by means of the hearer recognizing which illocutionary act the speaker intended to perform. Therefore the axioms for surface speech acts directly state the conditions under which the performance of the act will be interpreted as one illocutionary act as opposed to another. Cohen and Levesque (1980) have advocated a different approach by which the intentions behind surface speech acts are recognized. The basic idea is that the inference of intentions, given a speech act and some knowledge about the speaker, can be classified according to several patterns. It is these patterns of inference that characterize the illocutionary acts. Recognizing a particular illocutionary act as such is not necessary for achieving its effects.

If Cohen's approach were to be adopted by KAMP, it would probably result in minimal changes to the control structure. Illocutionary acts would still be retained in the abstraction hierarchy because they are still advantageous as a planning abstraction although not theoretically necessary. The ability of KAMP to plan indirect speech acts would be enhanced, because the different uses of a surface speech act would not have to be anticipated in advance and incorporated into the axioms, but of course the planner would have to expend additional resources to determine what the effects of the action are. The adoption of Cohen's approach would certainly require major changes to the underlying axioms. There are also some objections to this approach, discussed in Chapter 6. However, the ideas are promising enough to warrant further investigation.

8.2.2   *Formalizing action subsumption*

Also bearing on the issue of the relationship between actions at different levels in the hierarchy is the problem of a more rigorous formal description of action subsumption. Certainly the treatment of action subsumption by KAMP is one of the least well formalized aspects of the entire system. Currently, action subsumption is justified by Axiom 6.5, which states the effects of the use of a referring description to produce knowledge about the object referred to. There are two problems with this approach. First, the axiom refers only to knowledge, not intention communication. Therefore, an inform that is subsumed by a concept activation action does not really have the same effects as an inform, although it can possibly achieve the same goals. Second, the axiom is not used by the planner in formulating the plan, but only during the verification stage in which the plan is shown to actually work. The planner has heuristics embedded in the action subsumption critic about when action subsumption is desirable. The relationship between these informal heuristics and the axioms for action subsumption is not clear.

8.2.3 Enlarging the repertoire of linguistic actions

KAMP has gone farther than any previous analysis in extending a theory of action to levels lower than that of the complete sentence. This extension has been achieved by separating intention communication actions like informing and concept activation from more surface-oriented actions like asserting and describing, and attempting to connect the former to the latter. However, the effort stops short of achieving its ultimate objectives. There are many illocutionary act types and their relation to surface speech acts, including commissives, declaratives, and expressives, that have not been incorporated into KAMP's axioms or action summaries. Adding these actions to KAMP's repertoire will require fundamental research in representation of knowledge about concepts such as permission and obligation in addition to examination of the speech acts themselves.

8.2.4 Analysis of description identification and referring expressions

KAMP's analysis of referring expressions is extremely limited. KAMP is only capable of referring to objects about which the speaker and hearer share knowledge at the time the utterance is planned, and for which the speaker intends the hearer to pick out the individual to which he is referring. There are obviously many utterances that do not fit into this narrow mold. For example, attributive uses of definite descriptions are currently not planned, nor can KAMP plan to have a hearer use a referring description as an aid to gathering the information he needs to identify the referent. Because speakers frequently use descriptions that are not mutually believed with the intention that the hearer match the description to objects in the world to pick out the intended one, this is a large gap that needs to be filled.

One problem related to reasoning about the identification of referents is that

155

KAMP's representation of "knowing what something is" is insufficient to distinguish between having enough information to recognize the referent in a particular situation and being able to identify it in any situation. For example, suppose that in world W_0 agent A knows the referent of description D. That means that the denotation of D is the same in every world consistent with what A knows in W_0. Suppose that in W_0, D denotes P. Suppose that the next day, in world W_1, A is given another description D' that also refers to P. In that case D' also denotes the same individual in every world consistent with A's knowledge in W_1, and since the denotation of D' in W_1 is P, A must know in W_1 that he has identified the same individual in both cases.

Of course, if B requests A to deliver a letter to the man standing by the window, it is not necessary that A know that the man standing by the window is the same person he met on the street the day before in order to comply with B's request and hand him the letter. This unfortunate consequence is implied by the definition of knowing the referent of a description. It does not even depend on the use of rigid designators. It is obvious that considerable work needs to be done to arrive at a theory of description identification that does not have this flaw.

Identifying and characterizing the many different intentions that speakers may communicate by means of referring expressions, and exactly what it means for a speaker to intend a hearer to identify a referent constitute important areas of research in utterance planning.

8.2.5 Extended discourse

Although the theory behind KAMP deals with some discourse phenomena such as pronouns and other anaphora, it is silent on the important topic of planning and organizing extended discourse. KAMP is capable of planning short multisentence discourses, but there is no attempt to reason about the discourse as a whole, other than examining the plan for potential action subsumption situations. The discourses are coherent because each utterance is planned to achieve a top-level goal, or some related subgoal, and anaphora is used appropriately. However, no organization is placed on the utterances other than the left to right, top to bottom organization imposed by the plan.

In the case of complex goals involving a large number of propositions that the hearer is supposed to believe, this process becomes inadequate, and some type of higher-level organization is needed. One particularly promising type of higher-level organization is found in the form of discourse schemata (McKeown, 1982) and rhetorical structure schemata (Mann and Matthiessen, 1984). Such discourse schemata describe phenomena such as comparison and contrast, elaboration and explanation. It seems intuitively plausible, although there is nothing yet to support the conjecture other than intuition, that these discourse schemata can be treated by a planner as very high level actions.

Planning such rhetorical actions makes it necessary to explicitly represent the speaker's and hearer's beliefs about concepts such as the topic of the discourse and the relationship between propositions in a discourse. Rhetorical actions have a precondition that the speaker intends proposition A to stand in a particular relationship to proposition B, and the effect of such an action is to communicate this intention to the hearer. This analysis is highly speculative, but appears to hold promise for the treatment of extended discourse by an utterance planning system.

8.2.6 Efficiency issues

There are a number of issues concerned with how to make the KAMP theory useful in the design of practical computer systems. One important reason for the computational costs associated with KAMP is that KAMP takes into account a great deal of knowledge when it does its planning. It considers interactions between the various actions in the plan, and it carefully reasons about mutual knowledge when planning referring actions. The hearer's future actions and the adequacy of his current knowledge are taken into account when making requests. Humans seem to take these factors into account much of the time in planning utterances, so if KAMP is to behave competently, it must do so as well.

Given that a great deal of deduction is necessary for KAMP to consider all the factors that it does in planning an utterance, it is necessary to at least guarantee that the axioms and deduction system are as efficient as possible. There is a great deal of room for improvement in the current deduction system in this respect, and there are some interesting theoretical questions involved. For example, the current axiomatization of the possible worlds semantics of the **Know** operator makes very wasteful use of antecedent rules that cause a large number of irrelevant inferences to be made during the course of a proof. This problem becomes progressively worse as one must reason about the knowledge of an agent after a sequence of actions has taken place. The irrelevant inferences must be made for each state of the world between the initial and final states. The solution to the problem lies in devising a new axiomatization of the semantics that does not depend on forward chaining rules, but is still structured so that rules can be indexed and found quickly when needed.

8.3 Conclusion

Although much work remains to be done, the research on KAMP has made some important contributions to the study of computer natural language generation and the theory of communication. We are still a long way away from being able to pass the modified "Turing Test" cited in Chapter 1. However, the ultimate goal has been placed slightly closer to our grasp because now we have a framework for the design of a system that can plan utterances that satisfy multiple goals and that can take advantage of a variety of physical and linguistic actions in achieving its ends.

The research on KAMP has demonstrated the feasibility of the overall approach described in this book and illuminated a number of research issues that appear to be tractable problems for work in the near future.

Notes

1. This assumption is really much less restrictive than it sounds. It means that an agent knows the nature of the *immediate* effects of his actions, not that he knows all their logical consequences. In other words, an agent could know the effects of removing part A from part B, but be ignorant of the fact that part C is attached to part A. In the resulting state, the fact that C is no longer attached to the assembly is a 'consequence' of his action that he does not know, if we assume that it cannot be observed directly

2. There are other plans that might conceivably work, such as Rob's asking John to come into the hall at a specified time, and then telling him the date, instead of returning to the room. However, to keep things simple, we'll consider the two alternatives only.

3. Here we are dealing only with the reading of terms. One could also read object language predicates, and the treatment of the effects of such an action would be similar to the treatment of object language predicates in the informing action.

4. There are other universal preconditions that could be added, for example, that Rob knows who John is. It is unnecessary to add these preconditions because Rob, John, etc. are rigid designators, and it is assumed that everybody knows

who they are. KAMP takes advantage of this fact and only adds explicit universal preconditions for nonrigid terms.

5. Searle (1979) points out that not *all* illocutionary acts have propositional content. For example *"Hurrah!"* is an example of an illocutionary act with no propositional content.

6. The axiomatization illustrated in this chapter only outlines the most important aspects of the knowledge needed to describe requesting and informing. KAMP also requires axioms describing the effect of the actions on the speaker's private knowledge and intentions, and the knowledge and intentions of agents other than the speaker and the hearer. Tese details have been deliberately suppressed because they complicate the discussion without providing much compensating enlightenment.

7. The simple pattern specifications described here must be generalized considerably for other languages, particularly nonconfigurational ones. Kay (personal communication) has examined this problem.

8. The problems of associating lexical items with predicates have been deliberately simplified in this research. In general, there is no simple direct mapping from predicates to lexical items. Herskovits (1984) demonstrates how complicated this relationship can be for spatial prepositions.

9. Credit for the initial implementation of this deduction system belongs to Mabry Tyson.

Bibliography

J.F. Allen, *Recognizing Intention in Dialog*, Ph.D. thesis, Department of Computer Science, University of Toronto (1978).

J.F. Allen, C.R. Perrault, "Participating in Dialogues: Understanding via Plan Deduction," *Proceedings, Canadian Society for Computational Studies of Intelligence* (1978).

D.E. Appelt, "A Planner for Reasoning about Knowledge and Action," *Proceedings of the National Conference of the American Association for Artificial Intelligence*, pp. 131–133 (1980).

D.E. Appelt, "Problem Solving Applied to Language Generation," *Proceedings of the Eighteenth Annual Meeting, Association for Computational Linguistics*, pp. 59–63 (1980).

D.E. Appelt, "TELEGRAM: A Grammar Formalism for Language Planning," *Proceedings of the Eighth International Join Conference on Artificial Intelligence*, pp. 595–599 (1983).

J. Austin, *How to Do Things with Words*, (Oxford, New York, 1965).

K. Bach, R.M. Harnish, *Linguistic Communication and Speech Acts* (MIT Press, Cambridge, MA, 1979).

M. Berry, *Introduction to Systemic Linguistics: Structures and Systems* (Batsford, London, 1975).

M. Berry, *Introduction to Systemic Linguistics: Levels and Links* (Batsford, London, 1977).

L. Bolc, D. McDonald, eds., *Natural Language Generation Systems,* (Springer-Verlag, Berlin, forthcoming).

R.J. Brachman, "An Introduction to KL-ONE," in *Research in Natural Language Understanding, Annual Report*, Brachman et al. eds., pp. 13–46 (Bolt, Baranek and Newmann, Inc., Cambridge, MA, 1980).

G.P. Brown, "Toward a Computational Theory of Indirect Speech Acts," *MIT Laboratory for Computer Science Technical Report No. 223* (1979).

B.C. Bruce, "Belief Systems and Language Understanding," *BBN Technical Report No. 2973.* (1975).

W.L. Chafe, "Givenness, Contrastiveness, Definiteness, Subjects, Topics and Point of View," in *Subject and Topic*, Li, ed. (Academic Press, New York, NY, 1976).

W.L. Chafe, "The Flow of Thought and the Flow of Language," in *Discourse and Syntax*, Givón, ed. (Academic Press, New York, NY, 1979).

H. Clark, C. Marshall, "Definite Reference and Mutual Knowledge," in *Elements of Discourse Understanding*, A. Joshi, I. Sag, B. Webber, eds. (Cambridge University Press, Cambridge, UK, 1978).

H. Clark, "Responding to Indirect Speech Acts," *Cognitive Psychology*, Vol. 11 (1979).

P. Cohen, "On Knowing What to Say: Planning Speech Acts," *University of Toronto, Dept of Computer Science Technical Report No. 118.* (1978).

P. Cohen, C.R. Perrault, "Elements of a Plan Based Theory of Speech Acts," *Cognitive Science*, Vol. 3, pp. 177–212 (1979).

P. Cohen, H. Levesque, "Speech Acts and the Recognition of Shared Plans," *Proceedings, Canadian Society for Computational Studies of Intelligence* (1980).

P. Cohen, "The Need for Identification as a Planned Action," *Proceedings, Seventh International Joint Conference on Artificial Intelligence*, pp. 31–36 (1981).

E.J. Conklin, D. McDonald, "Salience: The Key to the Selection Problem in Natural Language Generation," *Proceedings of the 20th Annual Meeting of the Association for Computational Linguistics*, pp. 129–135 (1982).

C. Crieder, "On the Explanation of Transformations," in *Syntax and Semantics*, Vol. 12 (Academic Press, New York, NY, 1979).

B. Deutsch, "Typescripts of Task-Oriented Dialogues," *SRI International Artificial Intelligence Center Technical Report No. 146.* (1975).

K.S. Donnellan, "Reference and Definite Description," *The Philosophical Review*, Vol. 75, pp. 281–304 (1966).

J. Doyle, "A Truth Maintenance System," *MIT AI Laboratory Technical Report No. 521.* (1979).

D. Evans, "A Situation Semantics Approach to the Analysis of Speech Acts," *Proceedings of the Nineteenth Annual Meeting of the Association for Computational Linguistics*, pp. 113–116 (1981).

R.E. Fikes, N.J. Nilsson, "STRIPS: A New Approach to the Application of Theorem Proving to Problem Solving," *Artificial Intelligence*, Vol. 2 (1971).

C.J. Fillmore, "The Case for Case," in *Universals in Linguistic Theory*, Bach, Harms, eds. (Holt, Rinehart, and Winston, New York, NY, 1968).

C.J. Fillmore, "The Case for Case Reopened," in *Syntax and Semantics*, Vol. 8, Cole et al., ed. (Academic Press, New York, NY, 1978).

J. Friedman, "Directed Random Generation of Sentences," *Communications of the ACM*, Vol. 12 (1969).

G. Gazdar, G. Pullum, "Generalized Phrase Structure Grammar: A Theoretical Synopsis," reproduced by Indiana University Linguistics Club, Bloomington, Indiana (1982).

N. Goldman, "Computer Generation of Natural Language from a Deep Conceptual Base," *Stanford Artificial Intelligence Laboratory Technical Report* (1974).

H.P. Grice, "Logic and Conversation," in *The Logic of Grammar*, Davidson, ed. (Dickenson Publishing Co., Encino, CA, 1975).

J. Grimes, *The Thread of Discourse* (Mouton Press, The Hague, 1975).

R. Grishman, "Response Generation in Question-Answering Systems," *Proceedings of the Seventeenth Annual Meeting, Association for Computational Linguistics*, pp. 99–101 (1979).

B.J. Grosz, "Focusing and Description in Natural Language Dialogues," in *Elements of Discourse Understanding: Proceedings of a Workshop on Computational Aspects of Linguistic Structure and Discourse Setting*, A. Joshi, I. Sag, B. Webber, eds., pp. 85–105 (Cambridge University Press, Cambridge, UK, 1980).

B.J. Grosz, "Utterance and Objective: Issues and Natural Language Communication," *Proceedings, Sixth International Joint Conference on Artificial Intelligence* (1979).

B.J. Grosz, G. Hendrix, "A Computational Perspective on Indefinite Reference", (Unpublished paper prepared for the Sloan Workshop on Indefinite Reference, University of Massachusetts, 1978.)

B.J. Grosz, A. Joshi, S. Weinstein, "Providing a Unified Account of Definite Noun Phrases in Discourse," in *Proceedings of the Twenty-first Annual Meeting, Association for Computational Linguistics*, pp. 44–50 (1983).

H.W. von, W. Hoeppner, A. Jameson, W. Wahlster, "The Anatomy of the Natural Language Dialog System HAM-RPM," in *Natural Language Based Computer Systems*, L. Bolc, ed. (Hanser-MacMillan, Munich, 1980).

M. Halliday, "Language Structure and Language Function," in *New Horizons in Linguistics*, Lyons, ed., pp. 140–165 (Penguin Books, Harmondsworth, UK, 1970).

M. Halliday, *Cohesion in English* (Layman Press, London, 1976).

M. Halliday, *Language as Social Semiotic* (University Park Press, Baltimore, MD, 1978).

M. Halliday, J. Tastin, *Readings in Systemic Linguistics* (Batsford, London, 1981).

B. Hayes-Roth, F. Hayes-Roth, "A Cognitive Model of Planning," *Cognitive Science*, Vol. 3 (1979).

G. Hendrix, "Modeling Simultaneous Actions and Concurrent Processes," *Artificial Intelligence*, Vol. 4 (1973).

A. Herskovits, "Comprehension and Production of Locatives," *Berkeley Cognitive Science Report No. 20*, Universiy of California, Berkeley (1984).

C. Hewitt, "Description and Theoretical Analysis (using Schemata) of Planner: A Language for Proving Theorems and Manipulating Models in a Robot," *MIT Artificial Intelligence Laboratory Technical Report* (1972).

J. Hintikka, *Knowledge and Belief* (Cornell University Press, Ithica, NY, 1962).

J. Hintikka, "Semantics for Propositional Attitudes," in *Reference and Modality*, Linsky, ed. (Oxford University Press, London, 1971).

J. Hobbs, D. Evans, "Conversation as Planned Behavior," *Cognitive Science*, Vol. 4, pp. 349–377 (1980).

G.E. Hughes, M.J. Cresswell, *Introduction to Modal Logic* (Methuen and Co., Ltd., London, 1968).

D. Kaplan, "Quantifying In," in Davidson and Hintikka, eds., *Words and Objections: Essays on the Work of W. V. Quine*, pp. 178–214 (D. Reidel Publishing Co., Dordrecht, Holland, 1969).

R.M. Kaplan, J.W. Bresnan, "Lexical-Functional Grammar: A Formal System for Grammatical Representation," in J. Bresnan ed., *The Mental Representation of Grammatical Relations* (MIT Press, Cambridge, MA, 1981).

Planning English sentences

S.J. Kaplan, "Indirect Responses to Loaded Questions," *Proceedings of the Second Conference, Theoretical Issues in Natural Language Processing*, pp. 202–209 (1978).

M. Kay, "Functional Grammar," *Proceedings of the Annual Meeting of the Linguistic Society of America* (1979).

M. Kay, "Unification Grammar," XEROX *Palo Alto Research Center Technical Report* (1981).

K. Konolige, N. Nilsson, "Planning in a Multiple Agent Environment," *National Conference on Artificial Intelligence, American Association for Artificial Intelligence*, pp. 138–141 (1980).

K. Konolige, "A Deductive Model of Belief and its Logics," *SRI International Artificial Intelligence Center Technical Note No. 326* (1984).

R. Kowalski, "Logic for Problem Solving," *School of Artificial Intelligence, University of Edinburgh Technical Report No. 70.* (1974).

S. Kripke, "Semantical Analysis of Modal Logic," *Zeitschrift für Mathematische Logik und Grundlagen der Mathematik*, Vol. 9, pp. 67–96 (1963).

S. Kripke, "Semantical Considerations on Modal Logic," in *Reference and Modality*, Linsky, ed. (Oxford University Press, London, 1971).

S. Kripke, "Speaker Reference and Semantic Reference," in *Contemporary Perspectives in the Philosophy of Language*, French et al., ed. (University of Minnesota Press, Minneapolis, MN, 1977).

R. Lakoff, "The Logic of Politeness; or Minding Your P's and Q's," *Papers from the Ninth Regional Meeting, Chicago Linguistic Society* (1973).

J.A. Levin, N. Goldman, "Process Models of Reference in Context," *University of Southern California Information Sciences Institute Technical Report* (1978).

D.M. Levy, "Communicative Goals and Strategies: Between Discourse and Syntax," in *Syntax and Semantics*, T. Givón, ed. (Academic Press, New York, NY, 1979).

D.M. Levy, *The Architecture of the Text*, Ph.D. thesis, Stanford University (1979).

C. Linde, J. Goguen, "The Structure of Planning Discourse," *UCLA Artificial Intelligence Technical Report No. 9.* (1977).

C. Linde, "Focus of Attention and the Choice of Pronouns in Discourse," in *Syntax and Semantics*, Givón, ed. (Academic Press, New York, NY, 1979).

W.C. Mann, J. Moore, "The Computer as Author — Results and Prospects," *University of Southern California Information Sciences Institute Technical Report* (1979).

W.C. Mann, C. Matthiessen, "NIGEL: A Systemic Grammar for Text Generation," *University of Southern California Information Sciences Institute Technical Report* (1983).

W.C. Mann, "An Overview of the PENMAN Text Generation System," *University of Southern California Information Sciences Institute Technical Report* (1983).

W.C. Mann, "Discourse Structures for Text Generation," *Proceedings of the Tenth International Conference on Computational Linguistics,* pp. 367–375 (1984).

Z. Manna, *Mathematical Theory of Computation,*, McGraw Hill, New York (1974).

C. Matthiessen, "A Grammar and a Lexicon for a Text-Production System," *Proceedings of the Nineteenth Annual Meeting, Association for Computational Linguistics,* pp. 49–55 (1981).

J. McCarthy, P. Hayes, "Some Philosophical Problems from the Standpoint of Artificial Intelligence," in *Machine Intelligence*, Vol. 4, B. Meltzer, D. Michie, eds. (Edinburgh University Press, Edinburgh, UK, 1969).

J. McCarthy, M. Sato, T. Hayashi, S. Igarashi, "On the Model Theory of Knowledge," *Stanford Artificial Intelligence Laboratory Tech. Report* (1978).

J. McCarthy, "First Order Theories of Individual Concepts and Propositions," in *Machine Intelligence*, Vol. 9, B. Meltzer, D. Michie, eds. (Edinburgh University Press, Edinburgh, UK, 1979).

167

J. McCarthy, "Circumscription," *Artificial Intelligence*, Vol. 13 (1980).

L.T. McCarty, "Permissions and Obligations," *Proceedings, Eighth International Joint Conference on Artificial Intelligence*, pp. 287–294 (1983).

D. McDermott, J. Doyle, "Nonmonotonic Logic I," *Artificial Intelligence*, Vol. 13 (1980).

D. McDermott, "A Temporal Logic for Reasoning about Processes and Plans," *Yale University Department of Computer Science Technical Report No. 196.* (1981).

D.D. McDonald, "Subsequent Reference: Syntactic and Rhetorical Constraints," *Proceedings of the Second Conference, Theoretical Issues in Natural Language Processing* (1978).

D.D. McDonald, *Natural Language Generation as a Process of Decision Making under Constraint*, Ph.D. thesis, Massachusetts Institute of Technology (1980).

K.R. McKeown, *Generating Natural Language Text in Response to Questions about Database Structure*, Ph.D. thesis, University of Pennsylvania (1982).

J. Meehan, *The Metanovel: Writing Stories By Computer*, Ph.D. thesis, Yale University (1976).

R. Montague, "Syntactical Treatments of Modality with Corollaries on Reflexion Principles and Finite Axiomatizability," *Acta Philosophica Fennica*, Vol. 16 (1963).

J.A. Moore, W.C. Mann, "A Snapshot of KDS, a Knowledge Delivery System," *Proceedings of the Seventeenth Annual Meeting, Association for Computational Linguistics*, pp. 51–52 (1979).

R.C. Moore, G. Hendrix, "Computational Models of Beliefs and the Semantics of Belief Sentences," *SRI International Artificial Intelligence Center Technical Note No. 187* (1979).

R.C. Moore, "Reasoning about Knowledge and Action," *SRI International Artificial Intelligence Center Technical Report No. 191* (1980).

R.C. Moore, "Problems in Logical Form," *Proceedings of the Nineteenth Annual Meeting, Association for Computational Linguistics*, pp. 117–124 (1981).

J.L. Morgan, "Some Remarks on the Nature of Sentences," *Papers from the Parasession on Functionalism, Chicago Linguistics Society*, pp. 433–449 (1975).

J.L. Morgan, "Two Types of Convention in Indirect Speech Acts," in *Syntax and Semantics*, Vol. 9, P. Cole, ed. (Academic Press, New York, NY, 1978).

N.J. Nilsson, *Principles of Artificial Intelligence* (Tioga Publishing Co., Palo Alto, CA, 1980).

D. Perlis, "Language, Computation, and Reality," *University of Rochester Department of Computer Science Technical Report* (1981).

F. Pereira, D. Warren, "Definite Clause Grammars for Language Analysis — A Survey of the Formalism and a Comparison with Augmented Transition Networks," *Artificial Intelligence,* Vol. 13, pp. 231–278 (1980).

C.R. Perrault, P. Cohen, "Inaccurate Reference," in *Formalizing Discourse*, Joshi et al., ed. (Cambridge University Press, 1980).

J. Perry, "The Problem of the Essential Indexical," *NOUS*, Vol. 13 (1979).

M.J. Reddy, "The Conduit Metaphor — A Case of Frame Conflict in Our Language about Language," in *Metaphor and Thought*, A. Ortony, ed. (Cambridge University Press, 1979).

R. Reichman, "Conversational Coherency," *Cognitive Science*, Vol. 2 (1978).

R. Reiter, "A Logic for Default Reasoning," *Artificial Intelligence*, Vol. 13 (1980).

R. Rogers, *Mathematical Logic and Formalized Theories* (North-Holland, Amsterdam, 1971).

E. Rosch, C. Mervis, W. Gray, D. Johnson, P. Boyes-Braem, "Basic Objects in Natural Categories," *Cognitive Psychology*, Vol. 8, pp. 382–439 (1976).

S. Rosenschein, "Plan Synthesis: A Logical Perspective," *Proceedings, Seventh International Joint Conference on Artificial Intelligence*, pp. 331–337 (1981).

E. Sacerdoti, *A Structure for Plans and Behavior* (North-Holland, Amsterdam, 1977).

R. Schank, N. Goldman, C. Reigher, C. Riesbeck, *Conceptual Information Processing* (North-Holland, Amsterdam, 1975).

R. Schank, R. Abelson, *Scripts, Plans, Goals, and Understanding* (Lawrence Erlbaum Associates, New Jersey, 1977).

C. Scott, W. Clancy, R. Davis and E. Shortliffe, "Explanation Capabilities of Production-Based Consultation Systems," American Journal of Computational Linguistics, Microfiche 62, (1977).

J. Searle, *Speech Acts: An Essay in the Philosophy of Language* (Cambridge University Press, Cambridge, UK, 1969).

J. Searle, "Indirect Speech Acts," in *Expression and Meaning: Studies in the Theory of Speech Acts* (Cambridge University Press, Cambridge, UK, 1979).

J. Searle, "A Taxonomy of Illocutionary Acts," in *Expression and Meaning: Studies in the Theory of Speech Acts* (Cambridge University Press, Cambridge, UK, 1979).

J. Searle, *Intentionality: An Essay in the Philosophy of Mind,* (Cambridge University Press, Cambridge, UK, 1983).

S. Shieber, "The Design of a Computer Language for Linguistic Information," *Proceedings, Tenth International Conference on Computational Linguistics,* pp. 362–366 (1984).

C.L. Sidner, "Toward a Computational Theory of Definite Anaphora Comprehension in English," *Massachusetts Institute of Technology Technical Report* (1979).

R.F. Simmons, J. Slocum, "Generating English Discourse from Semantic Nets," *Communications of the ACM*, Vol. 15 (1972).

R.F. Simmons, "Semantic Networks: Their Computation and Use for Understanding English Sentences," in *Computer Models of Thought and Language*, R. Schank, K. Colby, eds., pp. 63–113 (W. H. Freemen and Co., San Francisco, CA, 1973).

M. Stefik, "Planning with Constraints," *Stanford University Computer Science Department Technical Report* (1980).

P.F. Strawson, "Intention and Convention in Speech Acts," in *The Philosophy of Language*, J. Searle, ed. (Oxford University Press, London, 1971).

W.R. Swartout, "Producing Explanations and Justifications of Expert Consulting Programs," *Massachusetts Institute of Technology Technical Report* (1981).

W. Wahlster, "Implementing Fuzziness in Dialogue Systems," in *Empirical Semantics*, C. Rieger, ed. (Brockmeyer, Bochum, Germany, 1980).

R.W. Weyhrauch, "Prolegomena to a Theory or Mechanized Formal Reasoning," *Artificial Intelligence*, Vol. 13 (1980).

R. Wilensky, "Understanding Goal-Based Stories," *Yale University Department of Computer Science Technical Report No. 140.* (1978).

R. Wilensky, "A Model for Planning in Complex Situations," *Cognition and Brain Theory*, Vol. 4, pp. 327–349 (1981).

T. Winograd, *Understanding Natural Language* (Academic Press, New York, NY, 1972).

T. Winograd, "A Framework for Understanding Discourse," in *Cognitive Processes in Comprehension*, Just, Carpenter, eds. (Lawrence Erlbaum Associates, New Jersey, 1977).

T. Winograd, "What Does It Mean to Understand Language?," *Cognitive Science*, Vol. 4, pp. 209–241 (1980).

H.K. Wong, "Generating English Sentences from Semantic Structures," *University of Toronto Technical Report No. 84.* (1975).